A GUIDE TO ADDITIONAL SOURCES OF FUNDING AND REVENUE FOR LIBRARIES AND ARCHIVES

British Library Cataloguing in Publication Data
A CIP record for this book is available from the British Library.

ISBN 0 7123 3307 X

ISSN 0263-1709

Library and Information Research Reports are published by the British Library Research and Innovation Centre and distributed by Turpin Distribution Services Ltd, Blackhorse Road, Letchworth, Hertfordshire SG6 1HN. In Japan they are distributed by Kinokuniya Co Ltd, PO Box 55, Chitose, Tokyo 156; and in New Zealand by Chivers (New Zealand) Ltd, PO Box 12096, Penrose, Auckland 6.

© The British Library Board 1997

RIC/G/326

Printed and bound in Great Britain by
Biddles Ltd, Guildford and King's Lynn

A GUIDE TO ADDITIONAL SOURCES OF FUNDING AND REVENUE FOR LIBRARIES AND ARCHIVES

Joanne Lomax, Susan Palmer, Graham Jefcoate and Stephanie Kenna

Library and Information Research Report 108

THE AUTHORS

Joanne Lomax left Lancaster University in 1994 with an MA by Research in Medieval Studies, the thesis for which was submitted as a multimedia computer application. This led to a post at the British Library as Assistant Project Officer on the pilot Universities Research Support Service. In Spring 1996 she joined the newly formed Electronic Libraries Development Unit at University College London.

Susan Palmer has been Archivist to Sir John Soane's Museum since 1989, having previously worked as an Assistant Archivist at the Greater London Record Office (now London Metropolitan Archives) for a number of years. She is Honorary Assistant Secretary of the Society of Archivists.

Graham Jefcoate is a Research Analyst in BLRIC with responsibility for the Digital Library Research programme. He had previously worked at the British Library in Early Printed Collections (Eighteenth Century Short Title Catalogue Project). He was Honorary Secretary of the Library Association Library History Group, 1990-1996, and was instrumental in setting up the Historic Libraries Forum in 1992.

Stephanie Kenna is a Research Analyst in BLRIC with responsibility for the preservation research programme and the heritage sector. She is secretary to The National Manuscripts Conservation Trust and the British Library scheme of Grants for Cataloguing and Preservation, and co-ordinates the provision of expert advice from the British Library to the Heritage Lottery Fund.

PREFACE

It was the earliest news of the proposed National Lottery that gave the Library Association, the professional body for librarians in the United Kingdom, the first impetus for examining the possible implications of the scheme for libraries. Ross Shimmon, the LA Chief Executive, attended a meeting at the newly formed Department of National Heritage on 1 March 1993 at which a number of official or semi-official bodies in the arts and heritage fields were represented. As a result of what he heard at this meeting, Ross Shimmon convened a meeting of special interest groups within the library sector to discuss an appropriate response.

A major outcome of the meeting at the Library Association in May 1993 was to propose a seminar on historic library funding that would review the proposed National Lottery in a wider context. This seminar was held on 18 October 1993 with the aim 'to explore sources of funding available for the preservation and promotion of historic libraries and rare book collections, drawing on the experience of fundraisers themselves'.

Inspired by the real enthusiasm engendered at the seminar in October 1993, a small *ad hoc* group of those present, including Susan Palmer of the Society of Archivists and the present writer, gathered in January 1994 at York Minister to review ways of taking the matter forward. At a meeting of the Special Repositories Group of the Society of Archivists in February 1995 I proposed that librarians and archivists should cooperate on the production of a brief and inexpensive guide to additional sources of funding. The proposal was well received and funding was obtained from the Library History Group and subsequently from the Society of Archivists. Matching funding was sought from the British Library Research and Development Department (now the British Library Research and Innovation Centre) to enable a part-time project officer to be employed to conduct the necessary research and collate the results. The present text is therefore substantially the work of Joanne Lomax, the project's researcher, with contributions from Susan Palmer, Stephanie Kenna and myself.

We should like to thank all the librarians, archivists and the administrators and representatives of funding agencies who have supported the project with their advice and who have made the production of this first edition of the *Guide* possible. Any errors of judgement or fact are of course entirely our own, and we should welcome any corrections, updates or improvements that might be usefully incorporated into any updated edition.

Graham Jefcoate, Library History Group

London, March 1997

CONTENTS

1 INTRODUCTION

A Guide to Additional Sources of Funding and Revenue for Libraries and Archives is a report of a survey carried out under the aegis of The Library History Group of the Library Association and the Society of Archivists, and funded by The British Library Research and Innovation Centre.

The aim was to produce a brief but comprehensive guide to sources of additional funding and revenue, providing a one-stop reference work for ideas, information and practical advice. Although we hope that the conclusions and recommendations in the report will be of wide interest, we have focused much of our attention on those with responsibility for smaller libraries and archives housed in historic buildings or holding special collections.

The need for such a guide has never been greater—core funding is becoming ever tighter and increasingly the available funds cover little more than the barest running costs. Special projects, conservation and even some staff costs frequently have to be funded by grants from funding bodies and trusts and this constant search for funds can seriously affect the everyday running of the library or archive.

While not claiming to provide the definitive answer to the problems faced by librarians and archivists, the *Guide* includes practical advice on how to plan and implement a funding application; concise information about the foremost national funding schemes and trusts; and a section giving information and advice about Lottery funding. Also included are ideas on how to raise extra funds through such schemes as Adopt-a-Book; how to offset costs through sponsorship; and how to make the most of volunteer workers and Friends groups. Ways of saving money through collaborative schemes are also explored.

The information has been gathered from information supplied by funding bodies and trusts, the personal experiences of the authors and from the results of a detailed questionnaire sent to over 500 libraries and archives in the UK and Ireland.

Among the major recommendations and conclusions of the *Guide* are:

- Libraries and archives proposing to pursue additional funding or revenue should consider organising the activity as a project, following some of the principles of project management methodology.

- A 'Project Initiation Document' might form a basis on which to plan a project and for drawing up a formal proposal for funding.

- The time spent planning the activity should, however, be in proportion to the task itself!

- It is essential to remain in close contact with the funding agencies throughout a project.

- Do not waste your own time or that of the funding agency with an application which does not meet the stated criteria.

- Present your application well: concisely and clearly.

- Sharing experiences with colleagues through participation in collaborative consortia or other forums is invaluable.

- The use of volunteers is to be treated with caution.

- Launching an appeal can entail considerable initial costs and consume much time and effort.

- The benefits of sponsorship need not be primarily financial.

- Publications and other items for sale must be carefully marketed to ensure a return that will cover the outlay.

- The effort put into fundraising must be measured against its rewards.

- Fundraising can be seen as a challenging and creative aspect of modern professional life in libraries and archives!

2 FIRST STEPS: SETTING UP A FUNDING PROJECT

In this chapter we assume that a librarian or archivist, or other responsible professional, has identified the need to seek funding beyond the limits of a normal institutional budget. We seek to give some practical advice about how this activity should be organised and managed using some of the techniques developed in the field of project management.

Additional funding might be needed for a range of reasons, including:

- Erecting new buildings or restoring existing ones;

- Improving storage conditions;

- Improving facilities and access;

- Conservation and/or cataloguing;

- Creating new or enhancing existing services;

- Collection development or exploitation.

Not all projects will need to consider every aspect of what is suggested below. Care should be taken of course to ensure that the time spent planning an activity is not out of proportion to the task itself! Any one of these might be the aim of a single project, but in practice funding will often be required for more than one at the same time. A project might therefore break down conveniently into a series of discrete activities. Alternatively, a number of projects might be regarded as stages within an overall programme.

Almost any institutional library or archive, whether in the private, voluntary or public sector, will at some stage need funding additional to its regular budgetary allocation. This need not necessarily be a wholly negative aspect of modern professional life: it could well be considered by the professional as a challenge, an incentive to think creatively and to broaden the range of skills he or she can bring to this (or any future) post. Indeed the successful management of a project of this kind will increasingly be seen by employers as a significant achievement in itself. The position of the library or archive within an organisation, and the professional with responsibility for it, will be significantly enhanced. This can only be a desirable outcome in a corporate world where libraries and archives are often considered peripheral activities and information professionals experience low status.

We will consider how some of the principles and techniques proposed by project management methodologies might provide a basis for planning and organising a project for which funding is sought. We will not suggest the wholesale adoption of any particular project management methodology, but we do feel that some of the techniques found in modern practice may be helpful. In particular, this kind of approach requires the prospective applicant to think in a systematic way about the activity for which additional funding is to be sought; to identify all the relevant factors; and to define aims, resources and timescales.

The justification for this approach could be set out as follows:

- It requires the applicant to consider all the various aspects of the activity and to organise them into a coherent plan;

- It provides a firm basis for a specific proposal or proposals;

- It demonstrates to grant-giving bodies that the applicant is well prepared and able to organise the work effectively and responsibly.

Even if the prospective applicant chooses a different approach to that outlined here, we hope this introduction will at least provide a checklist of points to be considered. Each of these points might reasonably be expected to be addressed in any formal proposal to a funding body. Indeed many of the funding agencies will issue guidelines or forms requiring information on these lines. A good example is the British Library Research and Innovation Centre itself.[1]

2.1 Getting Started

Before the prospective applicant considers an approach to a specific funding body or bodies, he or she might well begin by drawing up a document setting out the following:

- Aims, objectives and scope;

- Justification: making a case;

- Method;

- Management and quality assurance;

- Risks;

- Budget, costings;

- Project outcome and dissemination;

- Timescales; plan.

The resulting document (in project management jargon often called the 'project initiation document' or PID) can serve as a basis for internal discussions within an organisation and as a draft to be submitted to the appropriate authority (the governing body or committee) for approval. This approach will ensure that the activity has the support of the organisation as a whole at its highest decision-making level. It will also ensure that key players are identified as stakeholders at an early stage and provide valuable experience for the prospective applicant in formulating or presenting arguments. The draft document can be used as an information and reference tool and as a means of involving staff, supporters (and even users if appropriate) in the consultation process.

---

[1] See the Centre's *Guide to the Preparation of a Research Proposal* which is available in hard copy or on the World Wide Web at http://portico.bl.uk/ric/toapply/guide.html

In drawing up a document along the lines proposed and seeking its endorsement, the librarian or archivist will ensure that the organisation is aware of the specific aims of the project and has a stake in its success. By raising its profile, the library or archive might well move from the periphery to a place nearer the centre of the organisation. The proposal itself might be a useful way of showing that this apparently 'dormant' asset is not merely swallowing up resources but could be developed to raise the profile of organisation as a whole and to enhance and develop services. The securing of outside funding could in itself improve the departmental status of the library or archive within the organisation. This in turn could secure a more favourable allocation of internal resources in the future. It could also enhance the personal and professional position of the librarian or archivist.

The document drawn up will have a further, practical use: it may serve as the basis for formal applications, providing data and wording that could be drawn on for applications to individual funding agencies on an *ad hoc* basis as required. In adapting the 'source' document for specific use, however, care should be taken to ensure that the points raised by particular funding bodies are addressed specifically. Each may give different weight to different points or stipulate different criteria. A duplicated proposal dispatched to a number of different bodies is unlikely to be successful.

2.2 Aims, Objectives and Scope

Whatever approach is adopted, it will in any case be necessary to have a clear and agreed statement of the aims of the proposed project. This should form the first part of any document. It would be useful to consider the project within the overall corporate strategy. Does the organisation (as many now do) have a published 'mission statement'? Can it be shown that the proposed project will further this mission? If this can be demonstrated, it will strengthen the applicant's case in dealing both with internal decision makers and with external funding agencies. The professional should be aware of the potential value of the proposed activity to the organisation as a whole. Can it be shown that it will raise the public profile of the organisation to beneficial effect? Will it provide a basis on which further activities (including perhaps revenue-earning activities) could be built? Funding agencies will wish to see a project is soundly based within the organisation's own strategic planning and does not run counter to stated corporate priorities.

It will also be necessary to define the scope of the project closely. The applicant should consider whether the activity for which funding is to be sought is the subject of a single project or a series of projects. This could be achieved by breaking the whole activity down into particular areas—for example: building improvements, cataloguing, conservation, digitisation, and so on. These separate activities should be staged and allocated individual priority. This will enable the development of a proper plan and divide the project as a whole into discrete areas, the funding for which might appeal to different funding agencies.

The section on scope should also clearly state what is *excluded* from the project as well as included. This will avoid misunderstandings in the future and reassure funding agencies that the activity proposed is discrete, finite and realisable with the resources requested.

2.3 Justification: Making a Case

Any application for financial support or for the initiation of a specific activity within an organisation requiring the allocation (or re-allocation) of resources should be accompanied by a 'business case'. This will set out the justification for the allocation of resources to that activity. Too often library and archive professionals are reluctant to articulate the value and importance of the collections in their care. Neither should it be assumed that governing bodies or external funding agencies are themselves aware of their significance. Why is the proposed work important? What benefits will accrue? How will it further the aims of the organisation? Can it be demonstrated that the development of the asset that is the subject of the proposal (for example a library or archive collection) will add value to the organisation as a whole? It might actually be useful to list the negative consequences of any failure to secure additional funding: these might in some cases have an even more startling effect! A purely negative presentation of the case, however, is not to be recommended.

Applicants should not be reluctant to carry out a certain amount of background research, for example about the history and composition of a collection. This should demonstrate how it relates to other collections and to the work of the organisation as a whole. There are many ways in which a case might be built and presented. A collection of early printed books might be usefully compared with standard or specialised bibliographies. If it is possible to state that a significant proportion of a collection is apparently rare or even unique, this can only serve to strengthen a case. Archival collections might be of significance because they are particularly comprehensive or complete, because they provide unusual or valuable insights into historical processes and events, or because they are associated with key groups and individuals. The published assessment of independent experts should be cited where available. In some cases, such an assessment might be sought to strengthen the case.

If the applicant demonstrates in the application that bibliographical and historical research that underpins the case has been undertaken, this will certainly carry greater weight with funding bodies. Even the most obvious facts could usefully be stated or restated! Funding agencies might well consider the application alongside a range of different competing projects. What is it about this one that makes it stand out? Why should this project succeed where others might be rejected? A reticent approach is unlikely to succeed.

The application must also state the expected benefits that the successful completion of the project will bring the wider community. These should be broadly stated under four headings: **heritage, research, education and access**.

Heritage

Many funding agencies will ask if the collection or activity to be supported is a 'heritage asset' or of national, regional or local significance. This significance could be measured in comparison with other collections in terms of uniqueness, or rarity, or comprehensiveness, or completeness. A 'heritage asset' might be seen as an object or collection illuminating aspects of political, cultural, scientific, intellectual, economic or social history.

Research

How has the collection been used as source material for publication or research? Can specific work in progress or published work be cited? Is there a log or statistical overview of researchers using the collection? How will the activity for which funding is sought (for example cataloguing and conservation) promote research by improving access?

Education

Is the collection used, or of potential use, for educational purposes? The National Curriculum and adult education classes (or 'life-long learning' activities) are only two aspects that might be considered. Has the librarian or archivist discussed the potential exploitation of the collections with teachers or lecturers? Could the project potentially provide educational course materials?

Access

How will the successful completion of the project improve access to, and use of, the collections? What tools will be developed to enable that access? How will the collection be promoted outside the organisation? What terms and conditions of use will apply? Are people with disabilities considered? Will the project result in temporary exhibitions or permanent displays of significant material?

Does the project fit into any national or international strategy? Some applications might usefully refer to international, national or other criteria for 'heritage assets'. While the objects of most applications will not qualify for inclusion in UNESCO's World Heritage List, the criteria for inclusion as stated in the World Heritage Convention (1972) might provide suitable wording in some cases. Under the Convention, criteria for nominated properties should *inter alia:*

> Bear a unique or at least exceptional testimony to a cultural tradition or to a civilisation which is living or which has disappeared; or be an outstanding example of a type of building [...] which illustrates (a) significant stage(s) in human history; or [...] which is representative of a culture or cultures especially when it has become vulnerable under the impact of irreversible change; or be directly or tangibly associated with events or living traditions, with ideas, or with beliefs, with artistic and literary works of outstanding universal significance [...].

2.4 Method

Once the aims and objectives of the fundraising exercise are clear—and clearly stated—attention needs to be paid to the methods to be used in achieving them. A statement of these will in any case need to be made in any formal proposal. Funding agencies quite reasonably expect that a proposal will demonstrate the applicant's ability to manage the resources requested and to bring the project to a successful conclusion.

The methodology envisaged will of course depend on the nature and scale of the project and the resources available. Some agencies might expect large-scale projects to adhere to a formal project management scheme, this being seen as a necessary safeguard in the allocation of large resources. At present, this is more likely to be a requirement for large-scale building or IT projects but their formal application to other kinds of projects, for example heritage projects requiring considerable resources, cannot be excluded.

A document presented to a governing body should include some statement about the fundraising method or methods that are proposed. This will need to set out any funding agencies that are to be approached (with reasons for their selection). It should also describe other fundraising methods (from among the range described in this *Guide*) and again seek to justify the techniques suggested. In practice, many projects will need to describe a variety of complementary methods. It will not be possible to anticipate all the methods to be used at this stage and revisions should be made to the plan (with the approval of the project board) as matters progress and in the light of experience!

A proposal to a funding agency should set out the activities that will need to be undertaken to achieve the project's specific aims. The methods and techniques to be used should again be described and justified. They might include, for example, conservation methods or the application of certain cataloguing standards. Funding agencies will wish to see that the proposal demonstrates a grasp of the methodology proposed.

2.5 Management and Quality Assurance

In setting up any project (or indeed any organised activity), the question of how the resources are to be managed is clearly crucial and any 'project initiation document' must address this in detail. Firstly it should be established who within the organisation will be responsible for seeing through the project. Will there be a management board or committee? This might well be the case with major projects where considerable resources are to be managed. Normally such a group might be expected to include senior members of the governing body or administration and other (possibly external) experts. It might itself report to the organisation's own management committee and also, where appropriate, to the funding agencies themselves. Funding agencies may be asked for advice on who might be included; in some cases they will wish to nominate external persons directly. The functions of the project board will often be determined in accordance with local practice, but should be clearly stated in the proposal. Often they will include:

- Approving the project plan and any amendments;

- Taking overall responsibility for the allocation of resources;

- Monitoring project progress;

- Ensuring the project's successful conclusion.

A further advantage of such a board is to ensure high-level and collective support for the project manager within the organisation. It will also provide reassurance to funding agencies that the project has institutional backing and, where appropriate, formal access to external advice and expertise.

The day-to-day management of a project often lies with a single individual, normally the librarian or archivist themselves, a member of their staff or, with larger projects, a designated project manager (perhaps on a temporary contract). This person will be responsible to the project board or appropriate committee for the delivery of the project. The duties of a project manager might include:

- The detailed implementation of the project plan;

- The supervision of project or contract staff;

- The allocation of specific resources.

In some cases, an institution might have access to specialist in-house expertise or advice; in others, staff with appropriate skills will need to be brought in or work will have to be contracted out. Many funding agencies will require information about the qualifications and experience of any relevant project staff (including the supervisory board and managers) and contractors. This will normally take the form of *curricula vitae* appended to the proposal (or sent later where staff are to be appointed). They may also wish to see copies of temporary contracts.

The proposal should also state what checks and controls will be implemented locally. Will there be milestones or agreed dates on which the progress of the project will be assessed by the project board (and relayed to the funding body)? Funding bodies will often require the submission of regular, formal reports. Some will appoint formal external monitors to keep in touch with the project. They will wish in any case to be kept informed of progress on a regular basis.

2.6 Risks

In the nature of things, any project might encounter setbacks at any time during its existence. There will be any number of risks in any given project. Consideration should be given to ensure risks are kept to a minimum and that progress is checked against the plan. Careful planning and awareness of potential risks will help to avoid some pitfalls. Above all, mechanisms should be in place to deal with difficulties should they occur.

The personal circumstances of key project staff may delay progress and jeopardise holding to the plan. It might prove difficult to recruit suitable staff, for example when national schemes offer large amounts of funding to different projects simultaneously. This in turn might jeopardise the payment of fixed-term funding. A 'mix' of funding sources, through successful applications to different funding agencies, might complicate matters further. For example, some funding agencies will make their support dependent on specific criteria that cannot be fulfilled because of delays with other funding agencies. Some projects with complicated funding or staffing arrangements might prove so time-consuming to manage that little progress is made towards the actual objectives of the project itself.

Most funding bodies will be sympathetic to well-founded requests to revise project plans and the terms of grants in the light of changing circumstances. They should in any case be kept closely informed of difficulties (and potential difficulties) as soon as they occur. Concealing setbacks (or not reporting information about delays) is unlikely to be helpful.

Less tangible risks should not be neglected. For example, could the project and the resources required to see it through jeopardise the day-to-day running of the institution itself? Will staff be diverted from routine but essential duties? How will the new situation created by the project's successful outcome affect the continuing work of the institution? Will it require increased resources to maintain and develop further?

2.7 Budget and Costings

A plan will need to make a careful assessment of any factors in the project that will entail costs. Costing a project is therefore closely related to defining its scope.

The resources required to see the project through need to be carefully considered. Clearly the major items in many projects will be capital costs such as new buildings, shelving, bindings, restoration work and so on. But resources may also be needed to cover some or all of the following 'on-costs':

- Staff time and salaries;

- Overheads, such as space, heating, lighting, etc.;

- Research costs or contractors' fees;

- Equipment (including hardware and software);

- Postal, phone, fax and online costs;

- Relevant literature, photocopying;

- Printing and stationery;

- Meetings;

- Travel and subsistence.

All of these resources—and any others that might seem appropriate—should be noted even though not all will be required in drawing up a funding proposal to an external body. Some resources that are apparently without cost implications (for example, the use of voluntary assistants) will be found on closer examination to entail significant costs.

The formal proposal could usefully state what resources the institution itself was prepared to bring to the project (for example staff time, equipment, accommodation and overheads). Some funding bodies will require a commitment of partnership or matching funding. Others exclude certain categories of support (for example the purchase of hardware and software). Any preliminary work carried out—for example an assessment of conservation requirements—will need to be appended to the application with an indication of the cost of this initial outlay. Longer-term projects will need to take into account issues such as inflation.

Finally it is important to state clearly what financial benefits might be expected for the outlay proposed. Will cost savings be achieved in the long run?

2.8 Project Outcome and Dissemination

A list of the products that will be delivered by the project—often referred to as the project's 'deliverables'—should be included in any proposal. For example:

- Conserved and/or catalogued items or collections;

- Improved storage conditions;

- Improved facilities and access;

- New or enhanced services;

- Project reports, articles, monographs;

- Catalogues (conventional or online);

- New opportunities for research;

- New resources for collections development or exploitation;

- Greater expertise or awareness of the objects or collections involved.

These might usefully be listed and described briefly in an appendix to a project plan (see below).

The quantity and quality of information which projects disseminate about themselves is an essential part of their own justification. It should meet the needs of the funding bodies but also those of the organisation itself. A publicity plan could be drawn up in consultation with the institution's own press and publicity department (should it have one). Publicity about a new grant or donation may boost a subsequent appeal. Some funding agencies have detailed guidelines about publicity for their grants and for activities they support. They may in any case require applicants to draw up a strategy for the dissemination of information about the project's results and to include this in the formal proposal.

How information about a project is disseminated will depend on its size and scope but the following short checklist might be useful:

- A series of short statements of the aims, progress and outcomes of the project to be issued at the beginning and end, and at any significant point in between. These might usefully be accommodated on a single side of A4 or disseminated to email discussion lists. They should contain contact details for further information.

- Longer reports on progress for inclusion in relevant professional or other journals or for adaptation for use on institutional web sites.

- Full-scale progress or final reports are required by many funding agencies.

Consideration should be given to appropriate ways in which donors or funding bodies will be acknowledged in any presentation of the results of the project.

2.9 Timescales and Plan

Considering all the above, a plan with realistic timescales and costings should be developed. Working from the expected deliverables, a project might first be usefully broken down into stages. At the end of each stage a review of progress by the project board (in project management jargon often called 'milestone meetings') might be carried out. Within stages, staff working on the project will also need to meet regularly (or on an *ad hoc* basis) to discuss current issues. (These are sometimes referred to as 'checkpoint meetings').

The larger the resources required by the project, the more sophisticated the plan will need to be. Funding agencies might wish to be presented with a graphical representation of a complex plan in the form of a chart. An outline sample plan for a two-year library cataloguing project might be as follows:

1. Preliminary stage: months 1—3

First milestone meeting: Project Board meets to approve plan, including budget and procedures to ensure quality.

Project initiation: staff recruitment, training; purchase of hardware and software; initial bibliographical research; methodology tested; initial publicity planned.

Deliverables: approved plan; trained staff in post; equipment in place; methodology tested (e.g. x books satisfactorily catalogued according to the quality criteria agreed); contacts made with relevant sources of expertise (e.g. for foreign-language material, incunables, etc.); initial publicity.

Second milestone meeting: Board signs off the preliminary stage; adjustments made to plan where necessary, e.g. timescales, methodology, budget; funders informed of progress, changes.

2. Stage 2: months 4-12

Second stage: specific collections/categories of material catalogued; checkpoint meetings of project manager and staff to assess day-to-day progress; further 'problem' areas identified.

Deliverables: x books satisfactorily catalogued; journal article drafted; more contacts made; further publicity; manager's report to Board and plan for next stage.

Third milestone meeting: Board meets to consider manager's report; assesses progress in first year; signs off second stage; considers resources needed to tackle problem areas identified; approves plan for next stage.

3. <u>Stage 3: months 13-20</u>

Consolidation phase: most remaining books, including some problem material, satisfactorily catalogued; workshop organised; checkpoint meetings of project manager and staff to assess day-to-day progress.

Deliverables: x books satisfactorily catalogued; journal article published; workshop held; further contacts and publicity; manager's report to Board and plan for completion phase.

Third milestone meeting: Board meets to consider manager's report; assesses progress in second year; signs off third stage; considers resources needed to tackle problem areas identified; approves plan for completion stage.

4. <u>Stage 4: months 21-24</u>

Completion phase: remaining books, including problem material, satisfactorily catalogued; checkpoint meetings of project manager and staff to assess day-to-day progress.

Deliverables: x books satisfactorily catalogued; a completed catalogue (in the chosen format or formats); manager's final report to Board and draft final report to funding bodies; draft dissemination plan for project publicity; plan for post-project activities ('exit strategy').

Final milestone meeting: Board meets to consider manager's final report; assesses project outcomes and considers issues that will arise after project completion; approves final report for funding bodies and dissemination plan for project publicity.

This simple outline plan is unlikely, of course, to resemble any actual project plan. For example, the stages of a project might well run concurrently rather than successively. The outline does, however, serve to show the role of the project's board, the importance of agreed deliverables; and the function of regular checkpoint and milestone meetings.

2.10 Conclusions

In this chapter we have sought to demonstrate how fundraising activities might be organised within an organisation by applying some of the techniques of project management. We have suggested that prospective fundraisers might begin by drafting a simple 'project initiation document' for discussion within the organisation itself. Depending upon the size and scope of the project, this should seek to cover the points set out above. It could then form the basis for a formal proposal (or proposals) to specific funding agencies.

Many projects will of course be much less complex than the examples set out above and fundraisers will need to extract what is useful and relevant from the suggestions made. By adopting this general approach, however, fundraisers will demonstrate that they are aware of the great range of tasks associated with any such enterprise and can manage responsibly and effectively the resources they are seeking to achieve their stated aims.

3 SOURCES OF DIRECT FUNDING

3.1 General Principles

There are certain general principles to be observed when considering making an application for funding to a grant-making body or trust.

What earlier approaches have you made to the body, and, if any, what was the outcome? Some bodies stipulate that further applications cannot be made within a stated period of time. This will usually be made clear in their literature, or can be ascertained by an informal conversation with the Secretary. If the approach was unsuccessful, have you understood why? Just because an application has been turned down it does not mean that a fresh application will necessarily suffer the same fate, but clearly care should be taken to avoid introducing the same elements that caused the previous rejection. Keep copies of all previous applications, including unsuccessful ones.

What other current applications are there for the same project? Some bodies will not, or are not keen to, part-fund projects in conjunction with other bodies. Again, this should be clear from the literature. If, however, you are asked to state details of other current applications, do so: these should not be concealed.

Is your organisation or project eligible for the funding for which you are applying? Check carefully the stated criteria of the body or scheme to which you are applying: your proposal should be tailored to fit these. Be prepared to present your project in several slightly different ways if you are applying to several sources for funding.

What has been the experience of other colleagues in applying to this body? The pooling of experience amongst colleagues in one's own and related professions is invaluable, not only for those making the applications, but also for those responsible for giving advice on the subject, such as, for example, the Royal Commission on Historical Manuscripts or the British Library Research and Innovation Centre. If you are not sure who might have relevant experience to offer, try putting an appeal into the Newsletter of your professional organisation or, if you have access to it, on the Internet.

Do not waste the time of the fund-giver (or your own!) with an application that does not meet the stated criteria of eligibility, or that fails to provide all the requested information and in the requisite form. If you are uncertain, the Secretaries of most schemes welcome an initial informal telephone conversation about the proposal, to check that it is on the right lines and has some chance of success.

Present your application well. It should be brief and concise and organised in such a way that the specific points are clear and readily distinguished. You should also give a clear statement of the overall aim and a summary of the general points.

Brevity and conciseness should not, however, be achieved at the expense of clarity. Never assume that everyone shares your knowledge of the background to the application: spell out all the important things, even at the risk of stating the obvious. Do not, in the same vein, under-sell your case: make all the requisite points clearly and firmly but unsensationally.

Finally, be reassured: this all becomes much easier with practice! No one can pretend that fundraising is not a time-consuming business, but applications for grants do take a little less time once you are used to making them, and to the procedures and wording involved.

3.2 The Heritage Lottery Fund

The National Lottery

The fundamental aim of the UK National Lottery[2] is to raise substantial sums of money which will benefit five good causes—the arts, sport, the national heritage, charities and projects to mark the millennium—and make an important and lasting difference to the quality of life for people of the United Kingdom. The trustees of the National Heritage Memorial Fund have been given the responsibility for distributing Lottery funds to benefit the heritage of the United Kingdom.

National Heritage Memorial Fund

The National Heritage Memorial Fund was established under the National Heritage Act 1980 to provide, as a memorial to those who have given their lives for the United Kingdom, financial assistance towards the acquisition, preservation and maintenance of land, buildings, works of art and any other object which in the opinion of the Trustees of The National Heritage Memorial Fund is of outstanding importance to the national heritage. In practice, it has always operated as a fund of last resort.

Since January 1995 the Trustees of The National Heritage Memorial Fund have been responsible for distributing two funds: the Heritage Memorial Fund (the original fund) and the Heritage Lottery Fund. The Heritage Memorial Fund will provide financial assistance, in the last resort, for land, buildings and objects (including manuscripts and books) of outstanding interest and of importance to the national heritage and which have a strong memorial character.

Heritage Lottery Fund

The National Lottery etc. Act 1993 created a new and separate Heritage Lottery Fund[3] which NHMF can use to assist projects within its existing remit, but also in some important new areas:

- the construction of buildings and facilities designed to house or enhance public access to land, buildings or collections of importance to the heritage, and:

- the acquisition of items which are not themselves of importance to the national heritage (i.e. items of non-UK origin without previous UK associations) but which will complement a collection that is.

---

[2] Factual information derived and adapted from NHLF guidelines for applicants. Reproduced with the kind permission of the Fund.

[3] New legislation for the Heritage Lottery Fund is expected at the time of writing. The new National Heritage Bill will amend the National Heritage Act of 1980.

The primary aims of the Heritage Lottery Fund are to secure, conserve and improve assets of importance to the national heritage, whether land, buildings or objects, and to enhance public access to and enjoyment of such assets.

NHMF will consider projects falling within the whole range of its remit, including: ancient monuments, historic buildings and their contents and settings, designed landscape, land of scenic or scientific importance, special library collections, manuscripts, archives and other records, museum and gallery collections of all kinds, and industrial, transport and maritime history. Also supported are photographic, sound and film archives.

Who can apply for grants from the Heritage Lottery Fund?

Groups eligible to apply for support from the Heritage Lottery Fund are public, charitable or non-profit distributing bodies established in the UK and having the preservation or conservation of the heritage as one of their purposes. Private individuals and profit-distributing organisations are not eligible.

How much can be applied for?

Capital projects of all sizes can be considered. As a general rule, however, the Trustees will not normally expect to consider projects with a total cost of less than £10,000 unless an applicant can demonstrate both genuine need (in particular that there is no alternative source of public funding support) and the importance of the project to the heritage. The Heritage Lottery Fund will not provide 100% of the costs of any project. All projects should be supported by an element of partnership funding. In *Lottery Update* number 7 the element of matching funding was clarified: for grants over £100,000 normally 25% partnership funding is required, under £100,000 at least 10% matching funds are required, and for feasibility studies the level is around 25%.

If you are seeking a grant of over £1 million you should apply to the Major Museum, Library and Archive Projects programme. Separate guidance notes are available for this from the NHLF.

A new retrospective payment is now being made for work carried out in preparation for an application. However, applicants who are not successful will not be reimbursed for their investment in preparations for the application.

At the time of writing, the next round of applications (for bids of over £1 million) will be looked at from November 1997 onwards.

What are the Criteria for the Heritage Lottery Fund?

- Local, regional or national importance of the existing heritage asset or assets proposed for support;

- A clearly-defined 'capital' project, resulting in a significant advance for the heritage assets or the organisation concerned and not likely to be achieved without Lottery funds;

- Public benefit and accessibility (including access for people with disabilities);

- Quality of work proposed with regard to professional and technical standards, and historical integrity;

- Relationship to relevant local, regional and national strategies;

- Element of partnership funding;

- Applicant's need for financial support;

- Urgency of the project, where appropriate.

What projects can apply for funding?

Capital projects which are based on any of the following:

- Ancient monuments and historic buildings;

- Special library collections, manuscripts, archives and other records;

- All of the collections held by museums and galleries;

- Buildings, sites and objects to do with industrial, transport and maritime history.

The following types of project can apply:

- Buying, repairing, conserving or restoring buildings, land, objects or collections that are important to our heritage;

- Improving ways for the public to see any kind of heritage property. **Note that this includes cataloguing;**

- Projects which aim to improve the public's access to, understanding and enjoyment of buildings, land, objects and collections.

What projects cannot get funding?

Projects which are not related to a specific heritage item, for example, training schemes, regional marketing programmes, and general research projects cannot get funding.

Note that the Lottery does not currently give money for revenue only capital projects, therefore there are difficulties in making applications to raise endowments. However, the application from Chetham's Library, Manchester, and the application to buy the Churchill Papers both demonstrate that the NHLF will sometimes consider cases outside its published guidelines. Nevertheless, a very strong case would have to be made.

Heritage Lottery Fund Test: should you apply?

In brief, if you can answer yes to the following points your project may be eligible for funding:

- We are a UK-based public sector organisation, a charity or a voluntary organisation involved in preserving buildings or land or important objects or collections;

- Our application covers heritage based in the UK;

- The project for which we want support has not yet started;

- It is a capital project for one of the following:

    * buying property;

    * repairing, conserving or restoring;

    * new building work or improving buildings;

    * improving the public's access to, understanding and enjoyment of buildings, land, objects and collections.

- We will get funding from other sources;

- The total cost of the project is over £10,000;

- We have looked into other funding for our project and we think it is unlikely to go ahead without the support of Lottery funds.

Contact details:

Full information for applicants can be requested from:

The Heritage Lottery Fund
20 King Street
London SW1Y 6QY

Tel: 0171-930 0963

3.2.1 Checklists for Applicants[4]

Library and archive buildings: checklist for applicants

This checklist provides a pointer to the kind of information which expert advisors need to assess applications relating to new buildings, extensions and conversions of premises to house libraries and archives. It is not exhaustive and applicants may be required to

---

[4] These checklists were very kindly provided by NW James of the Royal Commission on Historical Manuscripts and S Kenna of the BL RIC—both of whom regularly advise the NHLF on applications.

furnish additional information on specific points. Applicants must also demonstrate that consideration has been given to a long-term strategy of collection management.

For all projects:

- Brief details of the constitution, history and development of the library, record office or other institution making the application;

- A statement of the objectives, subject scope, collecting policy, any restriction on use (e.g. for members only, fee for use), and its relationship with other similar institutions or collections;

- A description of the site and its context (including adjacent facilities and transport links), its history in brief and details of present ownership;

- Plans and drawings appropriate to the level of the application (full or outline) which show the size, mass, elevation and layout of the building, and details of the storage capacity and numbers of staff and readers who can be accommodated;

- An explanation as to why the extension/conversion/new building is necessary and what are the advantages and cost-effectiveness of the selected option over any other alternatives;

- Provision for the future expansion of the collections housed;

- Details of how the building will conform to relevant national and international standards and, in particular, of how the collections to be housed there will be protected against physical deterioration, theft, fire, flood or other disasters;

- Staffing levels needed to operate the library or archive as a whole after the completion of the project;

- Provision for the running and maintenance costs of the new building;

- Details of the relevant qualifications and experience of those involved in the project.

Applications involving repositories for archives and manuscripts:

- Details of any adoption of the Royal Commission on Historical Manuscripts *Standard for Record Repositories,* 1990.

Books, Manuscripts and Archives: checklist for Applicants

For all projects:

- A full description of the material which is the subject of the application, including an indication of its heritage merit;

- A copy of, or bibliographical details of, any existing catalogue, list or other description of the collection;

- An indication of the present and expected future use of the material concerned;

- A description of the conditions in which the material is or will be housed (e.g. type of shelving, temperature and humidity controls, security arrangements) and how far these confirm to relevant standards;

- A timetable for the various stages of the planned programme of work;

- A note of the relevant qualifications and experience of people to be employed on the project.

For preservation projects:

- A statement of the preservation aims and priorities of the institution and how the proposed project relates to these;

- A description of the condition of the material to be preserved or, if available, a copy of a conservation survey;

- A description of the proposed preservation work, including detailed estimates from at least one conservator.

For cataloguing projects:

- Details of existing catalogues, indexes or lists, and a description of proposed cataloguing or listing work including, as appropriate, details of hardware and software to be used, the cataloguing standards to be followed, the proposed means of dissemination (e.g. hardcopy, CD-ROM, via JANET etc.), and relationship with other cataloguing or listing projects (e.g. ESTC etc.).

3.2.2 Lottery Consultancy Firms

The (perceived) complex nature of Lottery applications has led to the growth of a new industry of consultants. They are able to advise on application techniques and have specialist knowledge of the process. The success rate of those firms who publish their results is remarkably high.

The advantage of these firms is that they can remove from the library or archive the need to learn in detail about the procedures of the Lottery application process. However, it is important to retain control of the project and not to allow it to become distanced from the people who will have to implement it. A consultant will never be as well informed about the substance of the project as the professional involved.[5]

The cost of employing a consultant will be beyond the reach of many smaller libraries and archives. However, it might be possible to claw back a proportion of these costs if the application is successful.

---

[5] The same proviso could be made about development officers within the organisation itself who are charged with drawing up an application on behalf of the library or archive.

A frequent negative remark about the Lottery in the responses to the questionnaires sent out in research for this report was that applications to the Lottery were a very complex and time consuming endeavour. To go through all this preparation and ultimately to fail would be a wasteful exercise—although these firms cannot guarantee success they can at least give advice based on experience.

We are not, at the current time, aware of any listings or specialist directories of such consultancies.

Case study (i)

Chetham's Library, Manchester

Chetham's Library, Manchester, is the oldest public library in the United Kingdom. It was founded by Humphrey Chetham in the 1650s and benefited from having a large portion of his fortune form its endowment on his death in 1653. However, poor early investments and latterly inflation had eroded the endowment until it was no longer sufficient to cover the running costs of the library and to undertake essential repairs. Chetham's was founded as an endowed library and as such it receives no government funding or funding from any other source except that which it can generate itself. Although the library was in dire need of funds it did not want to lose its autonomous status and so the endowment needed to be increased to a level where it could once again sustain the full functioning of the library.

In 1995 an appeal was launched under the patronage of the Duke of Devonshire to increase the endowment, make repairs to the presses, create a new reading room, establish a programme of conservation and to create a computerised catalogue.

A professional fundraiser was employed to take on the essential research and promotion work which an appeal of this scale would bring and she worked one day a week for 2 years. Her costs were borne out of ordinary funds and she has remained in the library after the receipt of the Lottery grant in order to administer it.

A glossy brochure was published, with professional photographs of the library and this formed the basis of approaches to charitable trusts. The appeal also received good publicity in the press, largely due to having the Duke as patron. By June 1995 the appeal had raised £200,000. It was around this time that the Heritage Lottery Fund came on to the scene as a major new source of funds.

Although the National Heritage Lottery Fund is primarily concerned with capital projects Chetham's desperately needed to increase the endowment; they therefore needed to put the case that the position of the library is almost undeniably unique in the UK and that by making an exception in this way the floodgates would not be opened to hundreds more applications of the same type. In order to persuade the NHLF to accept such an unusual application Chetham's needed to do some extensive persuading— papers were sent from Michael Powell (Chetham's Librarian), Nicolas Barker (former Head of Conservation at the British Library) and Fred Radcliffe (the former Librarian of Cambridge University and of John Rylands University Library, Manchester) which supported the view that this was the only way Chetham's could remain true to its founding ideals.

Once it was established that Chetham's would be able to apply for grant-aid the advisory process began. An advisory panel set up to brief the NHLF (including experts from the British Library and the Fund itself) visited the library, advised on the alterations and even recommended that the amount applied for be increased. Advice also came from other sources at each stage of the appeal and application—Michael Powell feels that Chetham's was lucky to have been able to call upon the expertise of the museum community who were, at the time, far in advance of libraries and archives in the skills of making funding applications. Chetham's is also registered as a museum and so they could call upon the Area Museums Councils for advice. Another concern was the vast amount of paperwork which was involved in securing the grant; it was in this area that the skills of the professional fundraiser were invaluable.

There were some concerns that because the NHLF works on a regional basis if any other large bids from the Manchester area went in at the same time as Chetham's there was a possibility that they would lose out. Fortunately this did not happen. The funding already raised through the appeal went towards the matching funding required by the Fund.

The Trustees of the NHLF announced its support for Chetham's in January 1996 with an award of £1,834,000. Before work on the capital projects could begin a contract was agreed, as is standard practice for NHLF projects. Negotiations over certain clauses were protracted and building work was delayed until late summer. The projects are being monitored by English Heritage and the British Library. English Heritage agreed to a monthly 'grant drawdown' system to facilitate cash flow. Regular visits were made to check the quality of the work. Requests for payments must be approved by the monitor before funds are released by the Heritage Lottery Fund; however, this only relates to the building works, not to the cataloguing or the conservation projects. Payments are made according to a percentage calculated at the award of the grant. The endowment portion of the grant was paid immediately following the acceptance of the award.

The starting date of the grant-aid caused some problems—there was a lot of preparation for the application which could not be claimed back because it had been incurred in advance and the NHLF did not make payments retrospectively. This included architects' fees and the costs of undertaking a pilot project for the building restoration. However, the NHLF has now changed its policy in recognition of the costs incurred by institutions in preparing their application, and 'sink costs' which can be clearly attributed to the capital project and which are incurred over the twelve months prior to the award can now be reclaimed as part of the main award.

3.2.3 The Millennium Commission and the Arts Councils

Two further organisations distributing Lottery funds should be noted here, although their direct relevance in the context of the present *Guide* is doubtful. Both the **Millennium Commission** and the **Arts Councils** are known to be potential sources of additional funding for libraries. The Arts Councils for England, Wales, Scotland and Northern Ireland have published different eligibility criteria but each will consider applications for capital projects. Each Council also operates with different procedures but all will respond to initial 'early warning' enquiries signalling an intention to seek funding. Partnership funding of at least 10% is expected. Applications are accepted at any time. In practice it is doubtful, however, if the Arts Councils would consider funding the kinds of conservation and cataloguing projects most historic libraries and archives would wish to pursue. There might of course be scope for seeking support for non-capital projects or elements of a project from the Councils, especially if they can be shown to be arts-related activities.

Contact details:

Arts Council of England
14 Great Peter Street
London SW1P 3NQ
Tel: 0171-312 0123

Arts Council of Wales
Lottery Unit
Museum Place
Cardiff CF1 3NX
Tel: 01222-388 288

Scottish Arts Council
12 Manor Place
Edinburgh
EH3 7DD
Tel: 0131-226 6051

Arts Council of North Ireland
Lottery Unit
185c Stranmillis Road
Belfast BT9 5DU
Tel: 01232-667 000

The **Millennium Commission** does not issue strict guidelines on eligibility apart from stipulating projects must enjoy public support and be 'lasting monuments'. Partnership funding must be at least 50% and applications are accepted in rounds. At present (spring 1997) it seems unlikely that a new round will be announced.

Contact details:

The Millennium Commission
Portland House
Stag Place
London SW1E 5EZ
Tel: 0171-880 2001

3.3 Other National Schemes, Charities and Trusts

Note that this section is intended to be a brief overview of the main funding bodies and is not meant to be exhaustive. Full details are available from the administrator of each scheme.

National Schemes

3.3.1 British Library—grants for cataloguing and preservation [6]

Since 1993 the British Library Board has again been making funds available annually to restore the scheme of grants for cataloguing and listing projects discontinued between 1989 and 1993. It also maintains the scheme of grants for preservation projects funded from 1986 to 1992 by the Wolfson Foundation. The sum of £125,000 per annum is currently available for this scheme.

The awards are administered by the British Library Research and Innovation Centre. For full details on applying please contact the Secretary.

Who is eligible to apply?

Any library or record repository may apply provided that:

- Reasonable access is allowed to members of the public;

- Suitable storage conditions are available;

- There is a firm commitment to continuing good preservation practice;

- Appropriate assurances are given for the reimbursement of the grant in the event of subsequent disposal of the material for which it has been made.

What material is eligible for grant-aid?

Awards are normally made for the cataloguing, listing or preservation of material which is of national importance and/or unique.

Priority will normally be given to the cataloguing or listing of collections not previously catalogued or listed, or only partially or inadequately catalogued or listed.

The following types of material are not eligible:

- Public records within the meaning of the Public Records Acts;

---

[6] Information taken from http://portico.bl.uk/ric/heritage/blgcpgde.html—a hard copy version of the *Brief Guide for Applicants*, which gives full details of how to apply, is also available. Reproduced by kind permission of the Secretary.

- The official archives of the institution or authority applying for a grant. Older records, particularly if they are unusual or unique survivals, may however qualify for consideration.

Grants will not normally be made for cataloguing or preservation work which has already been completed.

Projects from institutions funded by central government will only be considered for funding from this scheme where a newly acquired or non-core collection is concerned and the institution is not able to fund the project from its own resources.

Applicants are encouraged to contact the Secretary for further advice and informal discussion.

How much grant-aid is available?

Applicants are asked to bear in mind that there is considerable competition for limited funding and, as a guide, grants will not normally exceed £5,000. However, if funds permit, the awards committee will consider making awards up to a maximum of £10,000.

Applicants will normally be expected to contribute a proportion of the costs either from their own or other sources.

Grants will not normally be considered for projects costing less than £1,000.

What costs will grants cover?

Grants for cataloguing or listing projects may cover the cost of salaries and related expenses of staff specially employed for the project. They are not intended to cover capital costs or equipment.

Grants for preservation projects will be made towards the cost of repair, binding and other preservation measures, including microfilming, and towards the improvement of environmental monitoring and control. They may cover the cost of contract preservation and conservation or the salaries and related expenses of staff specially employed for the project, and expendable materials required for the project. They are not intended to cover capital costs or equipment.

How to apply

From the financial year beginning April 1995, closing dates for applications each year will be 31 January and 30 June, and meetings of the awards committee will normally take place a few weeks later.

Before offering a grant the awards committee will take advice from experts in the British Library, the Royal Commission on Historical Manuscripts, the National Libraries of Wales or Scotland, or other appropriate outside bodies on the importance of the material involved, the appropriateness of the application, the proposed form of conservation, cataloguing or listing, and the conditions under which the material will be kept and used. This will normally involve a visit to inspect the material.

Contact details:

Applications and all enquiries should be addressed to the Secretary:

Stephanie Kenna
The Research and Innovation Centre
The British Library
2 Sheraton Street
London W1V 4BH

Tel: 0171-412 7048
Email: stephanie.kenna@bl.uk

3.3.2 Higher Education Funding Councils: Non-Formula Funding [7]

The Joint Funding Councils' Libraries Review Group was set up in 1992 to review library and related provision in higher education in the UK. The Group produced what is known as the 'Follett' Report in December 1993. One of the recommendations of the Report was to '...invite bids from institutions for recurrent non-formula funding to support specialised research collections which are widely used by researchers in the humanities'. Two phases of funding were made available: non-recurring non-formula funding for one-off projects in 1994-95; and recurring non-formula funding for up to four years from 1995-96.

As a result, 327 projects at 66 Higher Education Institutions in the UK were funded under this initiative. Areas of the work covered with this funding include conservation, preservation microfilming, cataloguing and retrospective conversion of collections.

Although all funding is allocated for the current tranche of grants, at the time of writing, future funding within some of these areas of work has not been ruled out.

Additional information is available from:

Jacqueline Fitzgerald or *Rachel Bruce*
Research Collections Co-ordinator (NFF)   *Assistant Co-ordinator*
Library Office   *Research Collections (NFF)*
King's College London
Strand
London WC2R 2LS

Tel: 0171-873 2599   0171-873 2670
Email: jacqueline.fitzgerald@kcl.ac.uk   rachel.bruce@kcl.ac.uk

---

[7] Information provided by Jacqueline Fitzgerald, Research Collections Co-ordinator for the Joint Information Systems Committee (JISC).

3.3.3 The Museums and Galleries Commission/Victoria & Albert Museum Purchase Grant Fund [8]

The Museums and Galleries Commission/Victoria & Albert Museum Purchase Grant Fund is a Government Fund, which in 1997/98 stands at £1 million. The Fund, which has been in existence since 1881, contributes towards the purchase of objects relating to the arts, literature and history by local and university museums, art galleries, libraries and record offices in England and Wales.

It is administered by the Victoria and Albert Museum on behalf of the Museums and Galleries Commission (MGC). A parallel fund to assist in acquisition of objects relating to the natural sciences and technology is administered by the Science Museum, London (see below). Similar funds for both purposes are administered for institutions in Scotland by the National Museum of Scotland, Chambers Street, Edinburgh EH1 1JF.

In 1997/98 there is a ring-fenced sum of £50,000 to be used to support the purchase of manuscripts, documents and archival photographs. This 'M Fund' carries a maximum grant of 50% of the purchase price up to a ceiling of £12,000.

Purchases of more expensive archival material (and certainly all items costing more than £60,000) may be considered together with all the applications for museum acquisitions on the Main Fund. This carries a maximum grant of 50% of the purchase price up to an annual limit of £80,000.

Who is eligible to apply?

Museums and galleries, record offices and specialist libraries which:

- exist for the benefit of the public;

- maintain a permanent collection housed under museum conditions;

- provide an appropriate range of visitor services including regular public access.

Registration under the MGC scheme for museums and galleries is the basic criterion for application to the Fund. Those institutions not covered by the Scheme, such as libraries and record offices, will be investigated independently by the Purchase Grant Fund Office.

Applications **cannot** be accepted from nationally funded institutions or Friends organisations.

What is eligible for grant-aid?

- Any museum object or collection relating to the arts, literature or history priced at £500 or over. These might include archaeological, ethnographical and printed

---

[8] Information taken from material provided by the Fund to applicants in 1996—figures amended by the Fund for 1997/98. Reproduced with their kind permission.

material, rare books, objects illustrating social and popular culture as well as fine and decorative arts.

- Manuscripts, including estate maps, literary manuscripts, documents and letters with good historical content and archival photographs, priced at £350 and over.

How much grant-aid is available?

The maximum grant is 50% of the purchase price (exclusive of VAT) up to an annual limit, currently £80,000. The exact proportion of grant-aid awarded is subject to such factors as the availability of funds, whether the object is considered to be reasonably priced, the level of support from other sources and the comparative strength of the case made for acquisition.

Local commitment is vital to secure the support of the Fund. Grants are calculated at the rate of £2 for every £1 of local money raised up to the maximum 50% grant.

Advice on making a good application [9]

The V&A/MGC Purchase Grant Fund Office suggests the following hints for making a good application; many of the points are relevant to all funding bodies:

Consider the requirements:

- Do your institution and proposed purchase come within the Fund's terms of reference?

- Are you able and prepared to meet all the terms and conditions?

Allow maximum time:

- Contact **all** potential sources of help without delay, especially if you want to bid at auction;

- Submit applications in time to meet any deadlines.

Give the information requested:

- Complete the application form fully;

- Submit good quality photographs.

Make a strong case:

- Argue a full but concise case for the acquisition. Why do you need this **particular** piece?

- Don't assume knowledge or be afraid to state what seems to be obvious;

---

[9] Information from material sent to potential applicants to the V&A/MGC Purchase Grant Fund, reproduced with their kind permission.

- Remember that good presentation is important.

Get the best deal:

- Don't let enthusiasm for the item cloud objectivity;

- Seek advice on the price and get an independent evaluation if appropriate;

- Seek a museum discount;

- Investigate the tax advantages of private treaty sales.

Keep the Fund informed:

- How did you get on at auction?

- Have circumstances changed or have there been any developments?

- Claim the grant or let the Fund know if you don't need it.

Always ask if in doubt at any stage:

A telephone call can save all parties time.

Contact details:

Purchase Grant Fund Office
Victoria and Albert Museum
South Kensington
London SW7 2RL

Tel: 0171-938 9641

3.3.4 The Museums and Galleries Commission/Science Museum Prism Fund [10]

Purpose of the Fund

The Museums and Galleries Commission/Science Museum Prism Fund was established in 1973 to further the preservation, in the public domain, of items or collections important for the history and development of science and technology in all their aspects. Grants are available from the Fund towards the cost of acquisition and conservation of such material.

Who is eligible to apply?

- MGC registered museums;

---

[10] Information from *Guidelines for Applicants*, dated June 1995.

- At the Fund Manager's discretion, applications may also be accepted from charitable organisations engaged in the preservation of scientific, technological and industrial artefacts or monuments, although they may not be eligible for registration.

The following are **not** eligible to apply:

- Private individuals;

- Society- or company-run museums without charitable status;

- Nationally-funded institutions.

What material is eligible for grant-aid?

- Any movable object or group of objects illustrating the history of any branch of technology or science (including natural history);

- Archives and manuscript material with a significant technological, scientific or industrial content, but excluding books acquired for library or reference purposes.

Eligible costs

- Purchase price;

- The costs of dismantling, transport and re-erection;

- The conservation of material either on acquisition or from existing collections.

Note: Gross costs of less than £500 will not normally be considered for grant-in-aid

How much grant-aid is available?

- The maximum grant that can be awarded is 50% of the eligible costs, subject to funds being available;

- Grants are limited to £15,000 on any one item; £20,000 if the item is considered of exceptional significance;

- Aggregated grants to any institution are limited to a total of £20,000 in any one year;

- At least 25% of the remaining eligible costs must be raised locally;

- 25% may be found from other nationally administered grant-aiding bodies.

Contact details:

The Manager
PRISM Grant Fund
The Science Museum
South Kensington
London SW7 2DD

Tel: 0171-938 8005

Charities and Trusts

3.3.5 The Foundation for Sport and the Arts [11]

The Foundation for Sport and the Arts is an independent discretionary trust controlled entirely by its own Trustees. It is funded via the football pools.

The Foundation seeks, through the encouragement and funding of sport and the arts at every level to enhance the quality of life for the community generally. Rather than considering the pursuit of excellence as its main aim, the main objective of the Foundation is to support measures to increase participation in, and enjoyment of, sport and the arts by the whole community, regardless of levels of competence.

The Foundation ring-fences 60% of its disposable funds for medium and small bids. There is an upper grant limit of £150,000 for any single grant.

As an example of a recent grant, the British Library received £175,000 towards the cost of the Paolozzi sculpture to be placed in the piazza of the new Library building at St. Pancras.

The Foundation takes pride in dealing with applications swiftly and with the minimum of bureaucracy: its main concern its to 'identify worthy projects in sound hands, and put money in them'.

Contact details:

The Secretary
The Foundation for Sport and the Arts
PO Box 20
Liverpool L13 1HB

3.3.6 The Friends of the National Libraries [12]

The *Friends of the National Libraries*, a voluntary organisation consisting mainly of private individuals, was founded in 1931 in order to help acquire for the nation printed books, manuscripts and archives, in particular those that might otherwise leave the

---

[11] Information from information sent to applicants and from the 1995 Annual Report of the Foundation.
[12] Information from http://portico.bl.uk/services/national-libraries.html—reproduced with the kind permission of the Secretary.

country. The Friends operate by making grants towards purchase, by eliciting and channelling benefactions, and by organising appeals and publicity.

Among the earliest acquisitions with which the Friends have been associated are the Codex Sinaiticus and the Paston letters, both acquired in 1933 for the British Museum. In the succeeding sixty years, the Friends have helped many institutions, including national and university libraries and county record offices, to acquire several thousand items. Grants tend to be relatively small amounts for specific items.

Contact details:

The Secretary
The Friends of the National Libraries
c/o The British Library
Great Russell Street
London WC1B 3DG

Tel. 0171-412 7559

3.3.7 The J. Paul Getty Trust [13]

The J. Paul Getty Trust is a private operating foundation dedicated to the visual arts and the humanities. Through a museum, five institutes and a grant programme, the Getty provides opportunities for people more fully to understand, experience, value and preserve the world's art and cultural heritage. Through its activities and collaborative projects with institutions round the world, the Trust seeks to make a significant contribution to the vitality of the visual arts in the areas of conservation, scholarship and education.

The programmes of the J. Paul Getty Trust are the J. Paul Getty Museum, the Getty Education Institute for the Arts, the Getty Conservation Institute, the Getty Research Institute for the History of Art and Humanities, the Getty Information Institute, the Getty Leadership Institute for Museum Management, and the Getty Grant Programme.

Contact details:[14]

For general information email: publicaffairs@getty.edu

3.3.8 The Leverhulme Trust [15]

The Leverhulme Trust derives from the Trust created under the Will of the First Viscount Leverhulme who died in 1925. Included in the purposes of that Trust was the

---

[13] Information taken from http://www.getty.edu/gettrst.html

[14] At the time of writing, a recent announcement has stated that the Research Support grants programme has been suspended until January 1998; applications will be accepted again from November 1997. This is due to the Getty Institute for the History of Art and the Humanities preparing to move to a new building. The address for correspondence about the programme after this move will be 1200 Getty Center Drive, Los Angeles, CA 90049.

[15] Information taken from *Grants by The Leverhulme Trust: Policies and Procedures*, June 1996—July 1997. Reproduced with the kind permission of the Trust.

provision out of income of scholarships for such purposes of research and education, being valid charitable purposes, as the Trustees in their discretion might decide.

The income of the Leverhulme Trust derives principally from its shareholding in Unilever PLC and currently amounts to some £16 million a year. The terms of the Trust impose firm constraints on the type of purpose and mode of funding eligible for support.

The largest part of the income is spent on grants to institutions for original academic research. Awards are not offered for archival projects unless they involve or can lead to important and original research. The Trust does not award studentships in Britain.

The Trust is restricted to purposes of research and education. The Trustees may not make grants for any other kind of charitable purpose.

The Trustees are precluded from making capital grants for endowments, sites or buildings, or from giving grants for equipment. They cannot contribute to appeals or to core funding of other institutions or charities.

A **booklet** detailing Policies and Procedures of the grants given by the Leverhulme Trust can be obtained by telephoning 0171-822 6897 or email kfindlay@leverhulme.org.uk. General questions: telephone 0171-822 6938 or email josbourne@leverhulme.org.uk.

Enquiries and applications (grants to institutions) to:

The Director
The Leverhulme Trust
15-19 New Fetter Lane
London EC4A 1NR

Tel: 0171-822 6938

3.3.9 The National Art Collections Fund [16]

The National Art Collections Fund is Britain's leading visual arts charity. The Fund is an independent charity which receives no government funding. Grants are financed by the subscriptions of members, donations and legacies.

Who is eligible?

Any museum, gallery or other institution in the UK with a permanent art collection on public display may apply for a grant. A minimum requirement is registration with the Museums and Galleries Commission. Applicants must also be institutional members of the Fund.

---

[16] Information taken from *Information for Grant Applicants*. Reproduced with the kind permission of the Fund.

What is eligible?

Any work of art can be considered for a grant. The term 'work of art' is broadly interpreted to include a wide range of objects; for example, it includes architectural drawings and is therefore of relevance to libraries and archives. The quality of the work and its relevance to the applicant museum's collection are the principal criteria. The price and condition of the work are also important considerations, and, where necessary, an independent valuation or condition report may be required.

How to apply

The Committee of the National Art Collections Fund meets monthly to consider applications. Application forms must be submitted at least two weeks before the meeting, together with four clear black and white photographs of the object. The Grants Office can advise on dates of the meetings.

Wherever possible the Committee would like the item brought to the meeting for a viewing.

Grant offers

There is no fixed upper or lower limit to the size of the grant the Committee may offer. Applicants are expected to have approached other sources of help and, except in very special circumstances, museums are expected to make a contribution to the purchase from their own funds.

Contact details:

Mary Yule
Assistant Director and Head of Grants
The National Art Collections Fund
Millais House,
7 Cromwell Place
London SW7 2JN

Tel: 0171-225 4800

3.3.10 The National Manuscripts Conservation Trust [17]

The Trust was set up by the British Library and the Royal Commission on Historical Manuscripts, with funding from the Office of Arts and Libraries and from private benefactors, to provide financial assistance to owners and custodians in preserving the nation's written heritage.

---

[17] Information taken from the NMCT's *Brief Guide for Applicants* which can be found at http://portico.bl.uk/ric/heritage/nmctguid.html — a printed version of the Guide, with full application details, can be obtained from the Secretary.   Information reproduced with kind permission of the Secretary.

The awards are administered by the British Library Research and Innovation Centre on behalf of the Trustees.

Who is eligible to apply?

- Record offices, libraries and other similar publicly funded institutions including local authority, university and specialist record repositories;

- Owners of manuscript material which is conditionally exempt from capital taxation or owned by a charitable trust.

Applications cannot be accepted from institutions directly funded by the Exchequer.

What material is eligible for grant-aid?

Manuscripts, documents or archives which are the property of the applicant or required by law to be deposited on loan with the applicant (e.g. parish records under the Parochial Registers and Records Measure 1978) and of a national importance or significance which deserves special conservation treatment beyond the applicant's normal resources.

The following types of material are not eligible:

- Public records within the meaning of the Public Records Acts;

- The official archives of the institution or authority applying for a grant (older records, particularly if they are unusual or unique survivals, may however qualify for consideration);

- Photographic material;

- Audio-visual material;

- Printed material.

However, this is a flexible arrangement and if you are unsure whether to make an application the Trust would encourage you to contact the Secretary for further advice.

How much grant-aid is available?

Subject to funds being available grants will normally match the applicant's contribution and will not normally exceed 50% of the total estimated cost.

Projects will normally be supported for no more than three years.

Grants are not normally considered for projects costing less than £1,000.

What costs will grants cover?

Grants will be made towards the cost of repair, binding and other preservation measures, including reprography.

Grants may cover the cost of contract preservation and conservation or the salaries and related expenses of staff specially employed for the project and expendable materials required for the project. They are not intended to cover capital costs or equipment.

Grants towards the cost of arranging and listing manuscripts will normally only be available for making inventories or summary lists as the first stage in conservation.

Further details of the range, scope and extent of grants awarded are given in the Trust's latest annual report and accounts, which is available on request from the Secretary.

How to apply

The closing dates for applications each year are 1 April and 1 October and Trustees' meetings normally take place a few weeks later.

Before offering a grant the Trustees will take advice from experts in the British Library, the Royal Commission on Historical Manuscripts, the National Libraries of Wales or Scotland or other appropriate outside bodies on the importance of the material involved, the appropriateness of the application, the proposed form of conservation, and the conditions under which the material will be kept and used. This will normally involve a visit to inspect the material.

Contact details:

Applications and all enquiries should be addressed to the Secretary:

Stephanie Kenna
The National Manuscripts Conservation Trust
c/o The Research and Innovation Centre
The British Library
2 Sheraton Street
London
W1V 4BH

Tel: 0171-412 7048
Email: stephanie.kenna@bl.uk

3.3.11 The Pilgrim Trust [18]

The Pilgrim Trust was founded in 1930 by Edward Stephen Harkness of New York, with an endowment of just over £2 million to be bestowed on the urgent needs of the country of his ancestors, and to promote its future well-being. This fund has now grown to £40 million, and the Trustees make grants totalling about £1.5 million each year. Grants can only be made to registered charities or recognised public bodies for projects within the UK.

---

[18] Information taken from *Guidelines for Applicants* 1995-96. Note that new guidelines are expected to be issued for the year 1997-98.

The Trustees revise their guidelines and the headings for applications annually. New Guidelines are expected for 1997-98. As a rough guide, in 1995-96 they considered applications under the following headings (among others):

Art and Learning

- The acquisition of works of art and other objects for non-national museums, galleries and libraries;

- Repairs and improvements to non-national museums and galleries;

- Cataloguing and practical conservation schemes, including local community schemes;

- Support to individual scholars for the publication of learned works.

Preservation

- Buildings of outstanding architectural or historical interest.

What the Trust does not support

Grants are given at the discretion of the Trustees but are not normally given for:

- Appeals from individuals, or from bodies not registered with the Charity Commission or, in the case of Scotland and Northern Ireland, recognised as being charitable;

- Revenue funding; requests covering recurrent administrative costs, deficit funding, etc.;

- Activities that are primarily the responsibility of central or local government or some other responsible body;

- 'Mega-appeals' from national or non-national museums, i.e. schemes on which the comparatively small sums which the Trust is able to contribute would make no significant impact.

Contact details:

The Secretary
The Pilgrim Trust
Fielden House
Little College Street
London SW1P 3SH

Tel: 0171-222 4723

3.3.12 The Rockefeller Foundation [19]

The Rockefeller Foundation is a philanthropic organisation endowed by John D. Rockefeller and chartered in 1913 for the well-being of people throughout the world. It is one of America's oldest private foundations and one of the few with strong international interests. From its beginning, the Foundation has sought to identify, and address at their source, the causes of human suffering and need.

The Foundation works in three principal area: the arts and humanities, equal opportunity and school reform, and international science-based development.

The Foundation is administered by its president through a staff drawn from scholarly, scientific and professional disciplines. An independent board of trustees which meets four times a year, sets programme guidelines and financial policy, and approves all appropriations.

The Arts and Humanities

Grants in this area are given to support efforts to understand diversity and to bridge difference in culture, class, ethnicity and tradition.

Limitations:

As a matter of policy, the Foundation does not give or lend money for personal aid to individuals, contribute to the establishment of local hospitals, churches, schools, libraries or welfare agencies, or to their building or operating funds; finance altruistic movements involving private profit; or support attempts to influence legislation. In addition, the Foundation does not normally provide general institutional support or fund endowments.

Contact details:

The Foundation changes the emphasis of its invitation for applications regularly and therefore it is essential to obtain their full guidelines before applying.

The Secretary
The Rockefeller Foundation
420 Fifth Avenue
New York
New York 10018-2702
USA

3.3.13 Other Charities and Trusts

There is a vast number of charities and trusts in Britain, some with a national and some with a more local remit. For this reason it has not been thought practical to give details of all those whose scope extends to funding the arts, and more specifically historic libraries and archives. Instead a select list will be given of those known from the questionnaire returns to

---

[19] Information taken from http://www.rockfound.org/choices.htm

have funded relevant projects in the past. Not all of the trusts listed will, of course, be relevant to all projects.

It should also be noted that a number of these and other trusts will only give to registered charities, which will necessarily preclude many users of the *Guide* from approaching them.

The reader is recommended to obtain a copy of the current edition of *The Directory of Grant Making Trusts*, published by the Charities Aid Foundation.[20] It gives contact details, plus a brief resumé of the scope of the trust. It also has a very helpful section listing the trusts by the subject areas with which they are concerned.

Several useful publications are also produced by the Directory of Social Change:[20]

> *A Guide to Company Giving, 1995/96 edition*, edited by David Casson, London: Directory of Social Change, 1995 [new edition due Spring 1997]

> *A Guide to the Major Trusts, 1995/96 edition*

> Vol 1: the top 300 trusts, edited by Luke Fitzherbert *et al.*, London: Directory of Social Change, 1995 [new edition due Spring 1997]

> Vol 2: 700 further trusts, edited by Paul Brown and David Casson, London: Directory of Social Change, 1995 [new edition due Spring 1997]

Select list of trusts known to have funded library and archive projects in the past:

Contact details are taken from *The Directory of Grant Making Trusts* 14th edition 1995. The 15th edition for 1997/8 was due to be published as this *Guide* went to the press.

The Anstruther Literary Trust
Messrs. Bircham & Co.
1 Dean Farrar Street
London SW1M ODY
Tel: 0171-222 8044

The Baring Foundation
8 Bishopsgate
London EC2N 4AE
Tel: 0171-280 1000

The British Academy for the Promotion
of Historical, Philosopical and
Philological Studies
20-21 Cornwall Terrace
London NW1 4QP
Tel: 0171-487 5966

The Edward Cadbury Charitable Trust
Elmfield
College Walk
Selly Oak
Birmingham B29 6LE

The Clothworkers' Foundation
Clothworkers' Hall
Dunster Court
Mincing Lane
London EC3R 7AH
Tel: 0171-623 7041

The John S. Cohen Foundation
33a Elsworthy Road
London NW3 3BT
Tel: 0171-586 3192

---

[20] Address is given in Appendix 6.3.

O.J. Colman Charitable Trust
Child & Co.
1 Fleet Street
London EC4

Drapers' Charitable Fund
Drapers' Hall
Throgmorton Avenue
London EC2N 2DQ

The Vivien Duffield Foundation
Unit 3
Chelsea Manor Studios
Flood Street
London SW3 5SR
Tel: 0171-351 6061

The Esmee Fairbairn Charitable Trust
5 Storey's Gate
London SW1P 3AT
Tel: 0171-222 7041

The Marc Fitch Fund
2a Polstead Road
Oxford OX2 6TN
Tel: 01865-53369

The Gannochy Trust
Kincarrathie House Drive
Pitcullen Crescent
Perth PH2 7HX

The Goldsmiths' Company's Charities
Goldsmiths' Hall
Foster Lane
Cheapside
London EC2V 6BN

The Granada Foundation
Granada Television Centre
Manchester
M60 9EA
Tel: 0161-832 7211

The Heritage of London Trust
23 Savile Row
London W1X 1AB
Tel: 0171-973 3809

The Charles Hayward Trust
45 Harrington Gardens
London SW7 4JU
Tel: 0171-370 7067

The Headley Trust
9 Red Lion Court
London EC4A 3EB

The Idelwild Trust
54/56 Knatchbull Road
London SE5 9QY

The Leche Trust
84 Cicada Road
London SW18 2NZ
Tel: 0181-870 6233

The Manchester Guardian Society
Charitable Trust
Cobbett Leak Almond
Ship Canal House
King Street
Manchester M2 4WB

The Paul Mellon Foundation for Studies
in British Art
16 Bedford Square
London WC1B 3JA
Tel: 0171-580 0311

Mercers' Charitable Foundation
Mercers' Hall
Ironmonger Lane
London EC2V 8HE

The Monument Trust
9 Red Lion Court
London EC4A 3EB

The Rayne Foundation
33 Robert Adam Street
London W1M 5AH

The Reader's Digest Trust
Berkeley Square House
Berkeley Square
London W1X 6AB
Tel: 0171-629 8144

Royal Commission for the Exhibition of
1851
Sherfield Building
Imperial College
London
SW7 2AZ
Tel: 0171-594 8790

The Scouloudi Foundation
(Formerly the Twenty-Seven Foundation)
Hays Allan Accountants
Southampton House
317 High Holborn
London WC1V 7NL

Skinners' Company Lady Neville Charity
Skinners' Hall
8 Dowgate Hill
London EC4R 2SP
Tel: 0181-236 5629

The Wates Foundation
1260 Loudon Road
Norbury
London SW16 4EG
Tel: 0181-764 6000

The Wellcome Trust
183-193 Euston Road
London NW1 2BE
Tel: 0171-611 8888

Wolfson Foundation
18-22 Haymarket
London SW1Y 4DQ
Tel: 0171-930 1057

3.3.14 A Note on Funding Opportunities in Europe

Funding opportunities for libraries and information services offered by the European Union have expanded enormously in recent years and even the report by Peter Brophy published in 1995[21] is probably now in need of some revision. This remains, however, the best recent assessment. It includes a description of the relevant EC programmes with a report on a survey of attitudes to (and experience of) European funding opportunities by UK librarians in different sectors.

Brophy identifies a number of broad thematic strands under which funding for libraries is available:

- Research and development;

- Cultural programmes;

- Education and training programmes;

- Regional and structural programmes;

- Development programmes.

---

[21] Peter Brophy, *Opportunities for Libraries in Europe* (OPLES). Library and Information Research Report 103. British Library, 1995.

'Telematics' (the application of information technology) play a particularly important role in the European information policy development. There appear to be few if any current programmes aimed specifically at supporting smaller historic libraries or archives.

Even if relevant programmes were available, in practice it is unlikely that many smaller historic libraries would be able to find the resources to participate effectively in European programmes at this level. Respondents to Brophy's survey invariably mentioned the difficulty of accessing information about funding opportunities and about the amount of bureaucracy involved in participating in projects themselves.

3.4 Companies and Individuals

In this section we will look at the benefits of addressing unsolicited requests for various types of support to companies or individuals.

This is perhaps the hardest form of fundraising in that, because of the unsolicited nature of the activity, one starts with no premise of success. One may have to make a number of approaches for one successful one.

The appeal may be for money for a specified activity or for sponsorship in kind. The basic principles are, however, common to both requests.

Tailor your application very carefully. This type of approach by its very nature results in a high percentage of rejections: do not increase the percentage by blanket impersonal appeals and obvious circular letters. Even if you are trying the same basic approach with a number of companies or individuals, try and make the covering letter relevant in some way, however small, to each case. Always write to a named individual and personalise the letter where possible where there is an existing acquaintance.

Think creatively. Be prepared to think round your projects to see how they might be made to appeal to potential sponsors. If it is a cataloguing project, what sort of records are included? Do they throw light, for instance, on a local firm or industry?

If possible, break the project up into smaller sections. Rather than ask outright for the whole amount, illustrate what a range of sums from say £500 upwards will achieve. If the project in question is a cataloguing one you may, depending on the nature of the records, be able to target different individuals or companies with different sections of the catalogue depending on their interests.

Sponsorship in kind can be of various types. The most obvious are things such as specialist shelving or conservation materials. Consider, for instance, finding out whether a local photographic firm would sponsor some necessary reprography or help with an exhibition programme. If you have archive holdings which include family or personal papers perhaps these include bills for food or drink from old-established firms who might be persuaded to provide refreshments for functions over a period of time.

Always bear in mind that such giving is rarely, if ever, done entirely altruistically, therefore one of the first questions must always be 'What is the company/individual getting out of it?' If a catalogue or publication is being sponsored, the sponsor could be mentioned on the cover. Donors can also be acknowledged in any annual report produced. If books have been conserved, perhaps a special book-plate could be devised, though this will depend very much on the nature of the library.

Both companies and individual donors can get tax relief on their gift and increase its value to you through Gift Aid. Forms are available from the Inland Revenue.

Keep the sponsor in touch with the project as it progresses and invite them to see the finished result. They will probably expect there to be some sort of reception to mark the completion. If they are not going to finance this you may be able to get some sponsorship in kind from another source (see above). Send out press releases to local and national newspapers, radio and television stations as appropriate, and arrange for photographs to be taken. Be aware, too, of the potential of such occasions for increasing the profile of your part of the organisation within the wider whole: invite the chairman of your committee, head of the organisation, chairman of the trustees, or whoever, and introduce them to the sponsor.

Whilst needing to ensure that the sponsor gets something out of the deal, you must also be wary of individuals or companies wanting to get too much control. Both parties must be clear from the beginning what is involved, and this should be put on paper at some point. If you have serious misgivings do not proceed: it is not worth the money you receive if you or your organisation are compromised or it requires you to expend an inordinate amount of time or resources.

Some donors will wish to remain anonymous. There is nothing at all wrong with this, provided you yourself know the source of the money. Take the request to remain anonymous seriously, and be strict about not mentioning the name within your organisation; perhaps only the most senior staff need know the identity of the person concerned. Just because they have elected to remain anonymous, though, does not mean they will not want to be kept informed of the progress of the project.

Another approach to be considered is to suggest that people contemplate leaving your organisation a bequest in their wills. This could be done in literature about the organisation, in the Annual Report, in any newsletter or, where members are involved, by a letter to the membership.

You may have a historic building and/or collections which can be used to attract potential sponsors or generate income. Receptions for a carefully targeted audience can often be very successful, though it does need to be made discreetly clear on the invitation that this is one of the purposes. If there is a particular conservation or cataloguing project in need of funding lay out a display to be looked at during the evening, and have someone on hand particularly to show people around and talk about it.

Do not be afraid to spend some money on such events (if, of course, there is any to be spared). People by their nature like being flattered and pampered and an air of success breeds success. Obviously a nice balance has to be struck and overtly ostentatious expenditure avoided. Again, you may perhaps be able to get sponsorship in kind for the refreshments. Perhaps a local bar or restaurant much patronised by the staff and researchers would like to help.

If you cannot run to a reception, target people individually and invite them in for a glass of wine after hours. People love to feel they are getting something special and are seeing 'behind the scenes'.

If you have sufficient space to do so without endangering the fabric or the collections you should also consider hiring out the building or part of it for receptions or dinners. Clearly there have to be strict rules about numbers and procedures to avoid damage of any kind, but events such as these can be a useful source of income. Set the tariffs carefully after consultation: whilst you do not want to undersell the venue, nor do you want to make it so extortionate that no one uses it. Maintain an atmosphere of exclusivity as far as possible and make each group feel that they are privileged. Try to keep the building or collections a focus: the professional member of staff on duty overseeing the event might like to offer a guided tour or a short talk as part of the proceedings.

Sponsors could also be offered, as part of the benefit they reap, the opportunity to have one or a series of functions free or at a much reduced price. This is likely to appeal particularly to corporate donors. It can be useful for your organisation in widening your audience and bringing in more potential donors.

Pooling experiences and learning from colleagues is again invaluable. Bear in mind, however, that while people may be willing to share their experiences and ideas in general terms, they are less likely, in this particular area, to want to give away all their secrets.

This approach to fundraising is hard work, and the effort involved must inevitably be measured against the rewards. Except in rare instances it generates relatively modest sums, but often with some good public relations spin-offs. It is a useful part of the organisation's overall fundraising strategy.

4 INDIRECT SOURCES OF SUPPORT

The information in this section and in section 5 comes largely from a questionnaire sent out to over 500 libraries and archives. The themes and issues which were prevalent in the responses form the basis of these sections. The case studies were provided by a variety of different libraries and archives, some of whom requested anonymity.

The questionnaire is reproduced in section 6.2 below.

4.1 Collaborative Projects and Schemes

Case study (ii)

The Robinson Library, University of Newcastle

A useful co-operative project whereby Dutch library school students spent 6 months in the library on placement without cost ran for about 7 years and has just ended.

An accidental meeting in 1976 between the Librarian of the Robinson Library, Ian Mowat (then Librarian at the University of Hull) and a lecturer from the library school in the Hague led to the establishment of an annual placement scheme in half a dozen academic libraries in the north of England. This carried on until the Dutch government changed the funding basis for overseas placements last year.

It was up to each library to arrange its own placement activity but each gave a general undertaking to provide training as well as experience and agreed that the students from each library should have the opportunity to visit every other participant library as well. To some extent Newcastle tailored its programme to the needs of the individual student— e.g. if they were interested in the life sciences they would be given time in the Medical and Dental Library.

There were the inevitable hidden costs of staff time in training but these were more than compensated for by having a five/six month placement of students whose English was invariably excellent and whose commitment was usually high. The library also benefited by having an outside view of its activities.

At one stage Newcastle was taking two students a year but that proved too costly in the additional supervision time it required. However, the exercise did not require much additional setting up as the library is used to such activity—they receive a constant flow of placement students from the Department of Information and Library Management at Northumbria and so there was nothing unusual about what occurred (except for the length of the placement).

The Librarian states that he would recommend such schemes to anyone. There are already plans for a similar scheme involving Eastern Europeans being placed in many academic libraries across the north of England. Advantages seem to include the provision of a worker who is interested and able to learn and participate in the running of the library and who is going to be in the library for long enough for training to be of value. On another level developing links with overseas libraries is a valuable exercise and may lead to further useful joint projects. There is also the possibility that this new alliance may facilitate approaches to alternative funding agencies.

Collaborative projects are a useful means by which to avoid wasteful repetition of tasks between institutions. They can also provide institutions with skills or services which they do not have among their own staff. They can serve to expand the usefulness of a collection through reciprocal access agreements and so forth.

4.1.1 Collaborative Cataloguing Projects

Case study (iii)

An example of a collaborative cataloguing project is the scheme which operates between a university library, a cathedral library and a membership library.

The libraries are linked by access agreements which are of benefit to all parties—the University Library has access to the holdings of the other two libraries, some of which are of extreme rarity and value, and the two libraries themselves have their collections administered by trained staff who are paid by the University. The link between the University Library and the Cathedral Library has existed since the mid 1950s.

The merging of the catalogues of the University Library and the Cathedral Library (in the sense of their becoming part of the same computerised system) occurred when the University Library adopted a computerised catalogue in 1978. All Cathedral Library items catalogued or re-catalogued from then on were incorporated into the system. In 1994 an outside agency transferred the Cathedral Library items which had not yet been catalogued on computer from catalogue cards to computer records, and also transferred all the Membership Library card records in the same way, so it is from this date that these records were incorporated with the main computer catalogue.

In the case of the Cathedral Library, the only costs met by the Cathedral are those for the electricity which powers the computers. All other costs are met by the University.

In the case of the Membership Library much the same is true, except that the library is also making a relatively small contribution to the cost of installing extra terminals. (A larger proportion of the cost is to be met by the University, and the bulk by the National Heritage Lottery Fund).

The 'collaborative cataloguing' works reasonably well, considering the difficulties faced: the use of different classification systems; certain inputting and cataloguing errors; some technical difficulties; and the problem that the libraries themselves are on different sites.

Collaborative cataloguing schemes are of great value to libraries and archives for several reasons. The most obvious reason is the potential for sharing costs, particularly when implementing computer cataloguing. With computer catalogues, most libraries and archives choose to implement a system which uses a popular standard so that the catalogue can be made available on a network, maybe even on the Internet. It is therefore useful to join forces with other libraries and archives and to create a common catalogue, or at least one which can be accessed in the same way from each place. This is particularly useful when the units are each part of a larger parent organisation, for example a collegiate university; or where formal links already exist as within the example in case study (iii). Installing a framework for computer cataloguing can be expensive because of the need to use consultants and contractors, as well as the actual equipment costs. By implementing this framework as a consortium there is the potential to share the costs of the implementation and to negotiate bulk discounts on equipment. There is also the possibility of sharing the cost of maintenance or of employing a dedicated staff member to run the system.

A shared computer catalogue enables users at different sites to view the holdings of other libraries where they can use the collections. It can also allow the libraries involved to cut costs by not duplicating each others' holdings, if this is desirable.

Participation in large-scale collaborative projects such as the Cathedral Libraries Catalogue project or the English Short Title Catalogue (ESTC) should also be considered. The ESTC project now involves over 1500 libraries world wide, including many of the collections of historic material in the United Kingdom and Ireland ranging from large research libraries to small local archives. In recent years the ESTC has extended its remit to include all English-language printed material from Caxton up to 1800 (or material printed in English-speaking countries or colonial territories in other languages). It is thus building an online national retrospective bibliography.

Participation in ESTC involves reporting relevant titles to the ESTC team at the British Library (typically by supplying title page photocopies with a note of the pagination and physical format). These reports are then matched by the team against the master file and the collection's location symbol and the item's shelfmark are added as appropriate. Previously unrecorded items new to ESTC are catalogued by the team themselves.

This investment of effort brings a number of benefits to participating institutions. When the central team (and the contributing collection) are satisfied all the reported material has been matched and added to the online file, an output (in machine readable format, microform or printed on paper as required) can be supplied at cost. This allows the contributing collection to acquire the standard bibliographic records relating to its holdings in this field and to identify the rarity or significance of particular items. Recent examples of libraries that have obtained records in this way include Lambeth Palace, the Society for Promoting Christian Knowledge and the RSA.

For further information about contributing to ESTC, contact:

Richard Goulden
ESTC
British Library
Great Russell Street
London WC1B 3DG

Email: richard.goulden@bl.uk

The growth of the Internet has led to a culture where it is expected that catalogues should be accessible and collaborative schemes can allow less well off libraries and archives to become involved.

4.1.2 Collaborative Links and Consortia

Case study (iv)

Contract Conservator—Hackney Archives

Originally Hackney Archives employed a private conservator whom they paid less than the going hourly rate but compensated by providing tools and workshop space. Later a contract conservator was taken on instead—he works two days a week in-house for Hackney and is contracted out to other record offices or archives for the rest of the week. The contract work is carried out under the trading name of the London Borough of Hackney and the conservator is paid from the income. This allows the in-house work to be partially subsidised. The conservator is self-employed.

There are a number of well known examples of consortia, particularly in the field of conservation. Among the most notable of these are the links between Oxford and Cambridge colleges. Another example is provided by the RSA Library and Archive which has a very useful link with the Courtauld whereby conservation students work at the RSA on conservation projects. The RSA has no spare funding for undertaking a formal programme of conservation and so this has enabled them to conserve their small collection of oil paintings. It has also given the Courtauld students some real life experiences and problems to solve.

4.2 Sources of (Free) Professional Support and Advice

Many professional bodies consider it within their remit to offer advice to librarians and archivists who are looking into raising revenue. However, this advice is often given on a personal basis and they receive no formal recompense for it, so please bear this in mind when asking for help. Below are listed a few bodies which may be prepared to offer advice:

- The National Preservation Office;

- The Royal Commission on Historical Manuscripts;

- The Museums and Galleries Commission and Area Museums Service;

- The Library Association;

- The Society of Archivists;

- The National Heritage Lottery Fund lists statutory advisers who may be prepared to offer initial advice.

Librarians and archivists who have already made successful funding applications may be willing to share their knowledge—however, it is essential to ask politely and not to assume that they are honour bound to help.

The Historic Libraries Forum was established in 1992 to provide an opportunity for those working in smaller, historic libraries and collections to meet colleagues and discuss issues relevant to them (including, of course, funding). Membership of the mailing list is free of charges and the cost of participation in Forum events is modest. There is also a *Newsletter*.

To be included on the mailing list, contact the mailing list administrator:

Peter Hingley
Librarian
Royal Astronomical Society
Burlington House
Piccadilly
London W1V ONL

Email: pdh@ras.org.uk

Other societies and groups with an interest in the field include of course the Bibliographical Societies of London (and its sisters in towns such as Cambridge, Oxford, York and Edinburgh) and the Library Association special interest groups, especially the Library History and Rare Book Groups. Although membership of these depends on membership of the LA, participation in events is often open to all and is free or charged at modest cost.

4.3 Volunteers

Case study (v)

The Library of the Linnean Society of London

There are a total of 13 voluntary helpers. Four are members of NADFAS North Kent branch and all are retired ladies. Two of them have language skills, one is a classicist. They catalogue the reprint collection (handwritten entries on a record card, filed under first author in a separate card catalogue). The other two clean books and manuscripts from the Linnaean collection. They come for half a day every Thursday and the librarian has a schedule for the year so she knows who will be coming when. Their fares are refunded if they request it. The only preparation that needs to be made for their visits is warning of when they intend to come in so that books or manuscripts for cleaning or boxes of reprints can be got ready.

Five others are not NADFAS members and mostly come in one or two days a week and have specific projects that they get on with. All are middle-aged or retired ladies, mostly with a professional background or an interest in Natural History. The jobs undertaken include cataloguing the portraits and preparing listings, calendars and other work to help the staff find out what is in the archive and manuscript holdings.

The librarian needs to help them out sometimes and find new projects when a task is completed.

Another volunteer is a retired archivist who has been sorting and ordering an entire collection of conservation-related papers: she comes in by prior arrangement, usually to fit both her own and the librarian's schedules. Generally this arrangement works well and the librarian does not need to spend time supervising her.

Another valued volunteer is the retired Treasurer of the Linnean who, because of his trusted position, takes material home to work on, usually unsorted fairly recent archive material which he sorts and lists on his computer. He comes in once a fortnight on average to return results or collect new material.

Another is a botanical illustrator who comes in whenever she is in London, which may be every couple of months. She catalogues drawings and other illustrations and needs a few source books.

The final one of the thirteen is a retired teacher (and the librarian's mother-in-law) who has excellent filing skills: she comes in once every three weeks and files the catalogue cards for the reprints and/or anything else.

The staff do invest time in making their volunteer staff feel welcome, and to encourage this relationship they are invited to events such as the Christmas and summer parties. They are also given borrowing rights to books from the Library.

Most of the volunteers have been coming to the Linnean for many years. It has not been found necessary to check their work in detail but the staff do try to make sure that the work is correct while it is being carried out. Volunteers are also encouraged to ask for help if in doubt, and sometimes they help each other.

Recently the librarian has suggested some as DNB contributors and this has given them some welcome outside recognition. They are also encouraged to write up a short article on their work for publication in the quarterly 'Newsletter' which goes to Fellows.

Case study (vi)

Birmingham Libraries

At Birmingham Central Library volunteers are used to work on projects which the regular staff do not have opportunity to carry out. An example of this is the indexing of parish records—as long as the volunteer worker feels able and comfortable to read the handwriting used in the document, they can undertake this very useful task.

A very important project which the volunteers at Birmingham are helping to complete is the description and sorting of a collection of engineering drawings in microform. This collection encompasses over 100,000 items and was partially listed in the 1970s but was largely untouched until it was picked up again recently by volunteers. The library put an advert in a railway enthusiasts' magazine for volunteers who had a background in engineering and who lived in the area. To their surprise they were inundated with replies and eventually selected seven who now come in once or twice a week. These volunteers are overseen by a member of staff who works on this project for about one day every week—the investment of time was felt to be worthwhile because of the value of the work undertaken by the volunteers.

Volunteers are also used to undertake conservation tasks such as the dry-cleaning of materials. Another task requiring volunteers was the need to identify the views shown in items in the photographic collections—long time local residents were recruited to lend the benefit of their knowledge.

The types of people who volunteer to work in Birmingham Libraries are wide ranging and include ladies looking for something to fill their spare time, retired people (particularly engineers), students looking for work experience and people testing out library and archive work before opting for a career change. Those on work experience and career changers generally work for a concentrated period of time and are felt to give less to the library than a long term helper could.

This case study illustrates the Central Library Manager's intentions to use voluntary workers to bring in new skills to the workforce as well as aiding in the general running of the institution.

Case study (vii)

Guildhall Library, Manuscripts Section

In the Manuscripts Section of the Guildhall Library volunteers are currently working on a computer index of the late 17th and early 18th century probate inventories of the Peculiar Court of the Dean and Chapter of St. Paul's.

For the past two or three years up to two volunteers each summer have been taken on to work for a fortnight each on the project. The volunteers are selected from those who write to the Manuscripts Section asking about opportunities to gain experience before applying to an archive training course. Usually these people are nearing or at the end of their first degree and hoping to pursue careers as archivists. Volunteers are chosen initially from their CV and then by an informal telephone interview or, preferably, a visit to the library so that both parties can have a look at each other. The volunteers are initially only offered two weeks' work so that neither side is then committed long term if things do not work out. Fortunately, so far all the volunteers have been excellent and one or two have returned to do extra work on the project.

The project involves several elements: extracting information from the original probate inventories, checking other sources for cross-references and inputting the information on to computer, working on one bundle at a time. This provides sufficient variety and means that volunteers feel they are seeing the process through to the end. Each part of the work is carefully explained and the work gone through with each volunteer until it is clear that they are confident in what they are doing. Written instructions reinforce those given verbally. At the end of the fortnight each volunteer is given a printout of the work they have done.

The project is of mutual benefit. It gives the volunteers some of the experience they need and something to show for it, and it enables the library to tackle an important piece of work which it would otherwise not have time to do. The only problem is the time that the Deputy Keeper of Manuscripts (who supervises this project) needs to spend on the volunteers. She needs to be on hand to brief the volunteers and answer any queries, and to check their work as each step is completed. Owing to a lack of time to supervise them, only one volunteer will be taken on this year.

The comments made in the questionnaire replies suggest that the use of volunteers is an emotive subject. The attitude towards the use of unpaid helpers depends on a number of factors: the type of library or archive, the tasks that volunteers were expected to undertake and the skill level of the volunteer. It also depends largely on the amount of effort the institution is prepared to put into the training and supervision of its volunteers. A frequent comment was that they are a 'mixed blessing'—whilst their labour is often invaluable (particularly if there are insufficient funds to employ more paid staff) there is a feeling that they can cost more in staff time (for supervision, training, etc.) than the fruits of their labours merit. Volunteers are viewed with some suspicion, it would seem. Comments revealed a general fear that their work is inaccurate and that they take up a lot of time to supervise. However, since for many institutions it is their input which allows the library or archive to function, it would seem important to explore the ways in which volunteers can be employed to the best satisfaction of all parties.

An important note is that any institution employing volunteer staff must ensure that they have adequate insurance provision in case of accident, injury or damage to property.

An example of the formal use of volunteers is provided by the British Library itself. 'Voluntary Assistants' are often retired staff who are working on particular projects such as specialist catalogues and bibliographies for publication by the Library. Care should be taken that such activities would not normally be carried out by staff in employment: they should not be seen as ways of avoiding paying regular staff. As a rule of thumb, one should ask: 'Am I sure this activity, desirable as it is and of benefit to the institution, could not be carried out by employed staff during regular working hours?'

A perceived lack of motivation in volunteer workers was frequently cited as part of the reason why they are viewed so negatively by some. One of the questionnaire respondents even went so far as to suggest that paying students badly for cheap help was preferable on the grounds that they would tend to be more reliable and focused. Indeed, this is a difficult area for the employer of a volunteer helper—how far can one push the need for a volunteer to act as a part of the workforce? Should you just be grateful to have the opportunity to have an extra pair of hands, no matter how undisciplined or unreliable they are? Again this depends largely on the personal motivation of the volunteer and on the attitude of the employer—is the volunteer seen as someone to be indulged with some trivial tasks to keep them quiet or someone recognised to be working for the love of it and who should be rewarded with something fulfilling and suited to their skills? The questionnaire responses certainly seem to suggest that if some initial effort is put into the training of a volunteer and into making them feel part of the staff team then the value of this worker will increase.

The attitude towards volunteers differs in the different types of libraries and archives. Essentially, it seems that smaller libraries and archives make the most use of volunteers; generally the questionnaires suggested that in this setting they are valued highly and recognised to be a key part of providing a service. It seems that cathedral libraries and archives, in particular, depend on volunteers and one questionnaire even remarked that when the cathedral had come into more money and was able to employ more paid staff it caused a lot of friction with the volunteers. In record offices and local government archives volunteers, such as family history society members, often seemed to be assisting the office as a by-product of their own labour on their own research projects. In larger libraries and archives, there is a slight shift in attitude—volunteers are perhaps less vital to service provision and so the time they require in supervision becomes more of an issue.

Categorised below are some of the comments on volunteers which came out of the questionnaires.

4.3.1 Types of volunteers

On the whole, volunteer workers tend to be retired professionals looking to help out; unskilled but enthusiastic 'ladies of a certain age'; and work experience seekers. These categories are explored in more detail below.

Work experience seekers

> I am often approached by individuals interested in gaining experience of archive work prior to embarking on the archive diploma course. This can be useful for clearing up jobs that need the minimum amount of training but depends on how long the person stays, how much time they can put in and their aptitude for the work. In general having a regular volunteer who comes in over a longer period of time is probably more useful. (From a University Library).

A frequent comment about students wanting work experience is that they take up a lot of time for relatively little return. The library in the example given above has decided to combat this by only giving the students work that does not require much training. It seems likely that this leaves the students frustrated and does not really help the library much either. Work experience seekers are, by their very definition, untrained in library or archive skills and have volunteered their services in order to gain some real experience. The unfortunate truth is that these workers want to gain skills and then leave to use them elsewhere—some sort of compromise therefore needs to be reached. They are also viewed as something of a loose cannon—their skills have not yet been tested and they could prove to be a risk to the collection if not closely supervised. One comment which was echoed in a couple of questionnaires was 'we have been very fortunate with volunteers wanting work experience, but I wouldn't want them dealing with rare items'. Perhaps a programme of work shadowing would allow the student to learn while not interfering too much in the staff's daily routine.

One of the libraries which does not view work experience placement as an anathema— the Guildhall Library Manuscripts Section—has devised a standard 'drill' and treats them all the same. They are given specific finite projects and are normally on placement for a maximum of two weeks. This is explained in more depth in case study (vii) above. Presumably this would take some initial organisation but subsequently a minimum amount of effort would be needed to set up a timetable for each new person. It definitely seems preferable to have a pre-set plan about how to deal with volunteers and what to give them to do. It saves time in the long run.

NADFAS

Volunteer workers from the National Association of Decorative and Fine Arts Societies (NADFAS) were regularly mentioned in the questionnaire returns. These workers tend to be responsible, trusted and have often received training in basic conservation skills. Generally they form a very useful workforce in the library or archive. A comment on a questionnaire from a cathedral librarian sums it up:

> The training scheme for cathedral library volunteers is one run by NADFAS and covers the refurbishing of leather bindings etc. in the library. The people who stick with the work tend to be of mature years, female and enthusiastic, attracted by the artistic/skilled/useful nature of the work. Their rewards seem to lie in the fulfilment of the expectations which attracted them—seeing the results of their work on the shelves, and no doubt in the social benefits of working with like-minded people.

Contact details for the Association are in section 6.3.

Family History Societies [22]

There is a Family History Society in every county of the UK—they have over 100,000 members in this country and rely on record offices and archives to provide them with access to the material needed for their research. As a by-product of their wide-ranging investigations Family History Society members often contribute a lot of valuable work to the archive they are working in. They conduct extensive transcribing and indexing work—for example, through their efforts the transcription of the 1851 Census has now been completed. They also work jointly with the Mormons on some projects—for example, the microfilming of the 1881 Census; the Mormons usually contribute the funds to complete the project while the FHS puts in the research time.

Several of the questionnaires returned mentioned that groups of FHS members were currently transcribing parish registers. It is a standard practice for the FHS to present the record office or archive with any printed results which come from their research there and so there is a real benefit for them in return.

Members are not formally trained for the tasks but are supervised and helped by a project leader who gives guidance and informal training. All transcription or data inputting is checked fully before it is published.

---

[22] Information kindly provided by the Record Office Liaison Officer of the Federation of Family History Societies.

A comment made in another questionnaire was that, unlike regular volunteers, members of an FHS do not need supervision by a member of staff which removes one of the main objections to them: 'the Record Office gets the labour without needing to organise it'.

4.3.2 Tasks given to volunteers

Transcription and indexing seems to be a task given most frequently to volunteers in each of the different types of institution surveyed. It would seem that these vital archive/library tasks often cannot be covered by paid staff's time and so they move into the realm of the volunteer. It can be hazarded that these tasks are given to volunteers more because they are tedious and thus not favoured by regular staff rather than because they are particularly suited to the skills of the volunteers. On the contrary, both tasks require a certain level of skill and training to be performed well. However, if the task is seen as unimportant or menial the volunteer will not feel part of the staff team and will not be motivated to complete the task and do it well. A comment from an archivist seems to sum it up:

> Volunteer indexers have been used in the past but their enthusiasm tends to wane fairly quickly and it is difficult to check the accuracy of their work.

Transcription can be quite skilled work and would need thorough checking; the library or archive would then gain little from the exercise—the volunteer is given a task which the staff do not have time to carry out, but when it is finished the work must be checked or its completion will have been a worthless exercise.

Some volunteers are happy with tasks such as these and are very capable of doing them efficiently. However, this may well be due to factors other than the nature of the task. Giving volunteers a particular set task and allowing them to continue on it to its fruition rather than allocating diverse tasks on each visit will develop a loyalty and give volunteers a purpose to their work. This becomes even more valid when there is a very small paid staff and volunteer workers are expected to take the same professional attitude to their task as if they were being paid. The case study above provided by the Linnean Library illustrates this point. Having his or her own project creates identity and helps the volunteer to feel like part of the staff. By allowing workers to do the project at their own pace there is also no worry about forcing them to give more time than they have committed themselves to.

Volunteers need not necessarily be a source of unskilled labour—several of the questionnaires mentioned gratefully using the services of retired or unemployed professionals. A comment from the Central Library Manager of Birmingham Libraries, who provided the case study above, shows how volunteers can bring specific skills needed for a project:

> Generally we are seeking to bring in skills or background knowledge from the community that staff do not possess, and/or to conduct much more detailed investigations that staff time would not permit.

This is very valid point—volunteers can be a very useful supplementary workforce. The comment about conducting detailed investigations is particularly relevant when staff are pared down to subsistence level through a shortage of funds. If volunteers are able to carry out the investigations for, for example, a funding proposal, then this could offset some of the costs of making the proposal. A frequent comment on the questionnaires was that although the money that could come from a grant application was desperately needed there was no spare time in the working week for a good proposal to be properly formulated. However, this would be a task for a very special and trusted volunteer.

As for volunteers in general, who may be interested in any aspect of library work and not just in treating bindings, it could be said that they are mainly middle-class people interested in/attracted by/skilled in library/archive or related work. If they can be left to get on with their work and do it properly and accurately after a minimum of guidance, they can be very valuable, but this is not necessarily the case. The library or archive cannot expect to get valuable returns unless it is prepared to put time and effort into training and supervision.

5 ALTERNATIVE REVENUE GENERATION SCHEMES

This chapter uses the responses made in the questionnaire to suggest ways of generating revenue either for special projects or purchases or to cover some of the recurrent costs of the library or archive.

Many questionnaires mentioned that revenue generation schemes often lost momentum and generally ran out of steam after a certain period of time. This is only natural, but a decision must be made as to whether to close this scheme and start another or to re-generate it. Do not be discouraged by this experience.

5.1 Appeals

Case study (viii)

A fellow of the college bequeathed some 2000 books in 1989 but there was nowhere to house them within the library. When the new librarian took over a few years later the idea of raising money through an appeal grew—the aim was to turn the disused basement of the library into useful library space and create a browsing area where the bequeathed collection could be housed.

It was decided to contact alumni of the college who had known the benefactor to ask for donations towards the conversion work. The alumni office and senior members of staff from the benefactor's department spent some time making up the list of known friends and associates. The money was eventually raised and the basement converted.

However, with hindsight, the librarian realises that this may not have been the most cost-effective way of raising the funds. She was approached after the conclusion of the appeal by people who said they would have given money to the library appeal had they known about it. It would also seem that the time and effort taken to make up the select list could have paid for a much larger mailshot which would have resulted in more funds coming in.

The librarian advises that there is a need to think very carefully about the target audience of an appeal—in this case the appeal had interest to a wider audience than was approached. However, if it had been intended only to create a reading area for the bequeathed books rather than a general amenity for the library this narrow approach would have been most suitable.

Case study (ix)

This library made an appeal to assist in the purchase of an important collection of letters written by a well known literary figure. At the time there was very little money to use on purchases of this type, even with the help of matching grants from sources such as the V&A/MGC Purchase Grant Fund. The library was also very short of time, having only a matter of weeks before the collection was due to be auctioned. By chance, the event coincided with the formation of their Friends group. They were therefore able to gain a two-way advantage: the need to rapidly raise funds acted as a vehicle to attract membership; and the members helped to raise further funds. As an incentive, life membership of the Friends was offered at a reduced rate as a means of raising a large initial sum. Lists of potential donors were compiled who were approached and invited to pledge funds towards the cost of purchasing the letters. In the event, sufficient funds and pledges were raised to cover a bid of two and a half times the amount actually paid.

The widespread nature of this appeal, which inevitably attracted much press interest, led to the concern that it would simultaneously be raising interest in the auction, perhaps alerting other potential bidders (particularly from overseas) to the importance of the collection. As it turned out, there was very little opposition at the auction so their initial fears may have been misplaced. However, the massive publicity resulting from this success does appear to have contributed to attracting greater interest from other (particularly foreign) institutions at subsequent auctions and private sales of other collections by the same writer.

Running an appeal depends very heavily on the institution and on its objectives. This section tries to pull together a few of the ideas which came out of the questionnaire responses but is deliberately not as detailed as other sections.

Appeals now seem to be an everyday part of library and archive business—as core funding falls towards crisis levels, projects which fall outside core activity and unexpected occurrences or opportunities need to be funded by outside agencies. If a project, purchase or disaster is not covered or not fundable by any of the funding bodies then an appeal may be the only route available. Conversely, by running an appeal as the first choice activity the institution may seek to raise awareness of its plight along with funds.

It is important to stress that appeals can cost large sums of money; indeed it can be argued that if an appeal is planned thoroughly and carried out well it will definitely incur substantial costs. A major cost is the time that needs to be put into the research and preparation of an appeal. Many of the large scale appeals which were mentioned in the returned questionnaires had appointed appeals administrators or professional fundraisers to organise both the endless paperwork and the preparatory research. The costs of this person need to be met, at least to begin with, from the ordinary funds of the library or archive. At the very least if the appeal is being run by a regular member of staff this person's time needs to be compensated for. It is an unfortunate truth that the phrase which was repeated with alarming regularity in the questionnaires was that 'it takes money to make money'.

Setting up an appeal committee will help to spread the workload and bring in new contacts and ideas. Asking well known local figures to be involved will also give the appeal a certain kudos or respectability. If the appeal is going to approach local businesses and community groups then it may well be of value to involve members of those groups in the planning of the appeal by appointing them to the appeal committee. This gives the appeal a way in which to make contact with its target groups. An example of this is the archive which needed to raise funds to purchase a collection of papers; the letters sent out to the chosen targets were personalised by a member of the local gentry. Although the recipients of the letter may not have been very familiar with the archive they would have known the name in the signature and it is to be hoped that they will have supported the purchase because of his or her involvement.

An exhibition or open day to showcase the library, archive or item which is the object of the appeal will serve to increase public and media interest and possibly raise money. It will also show potential donors that the object is worth conserving or saving or that the collection will be enhanced by the purchase of the new item. It will also prepare the ground for the audience of the appeal—they will have at least a little background knowledge about the project.

It is worth spending money on good quality promotional literature. The appeals officer at Chetham's Library, Manchester, said that having professional colour photographs of the library taken for the appeal brochure was invaluable as the picture indisputably told a thousand words. (For details of the Chetham's Appeal see case study (i).)

Appeals do not have to be widespread and public. Several of the questionnaires mentioned circumstances where they felt it more appropriate to ask for funds only from certain sections of the community, for example local businesses. Arguably, this reduction in scale would lead to a similar reduction in costs but a certain level of funds would need to be invested in the appeal in terms of time and publicity because it would still be important to be well prepared. A comment of value in this situation is this from a large local studies archive:

> We targeted the appeal to the local business community, which has been very supportive, especially of work in connection with our industrial collections. We have found that it is best to work with an insider in the business community rather than to cold call.

The nature of the appeal will, of course, depend on its objectives. Scaling the appeal to its probable benefactors is a delicate and skilled task.

Where material is held by a library or archive on deposit approaches are often made to the owners of this material, particularly for conservation exercises and exhibitions. The advantage here would be that the owners of the material have a vested interest in making sure that the collection is treated well.

Several of the libraries and archives which have a membership system mentioned that they made appeals to their members in the first instance before taking it wider. Universities, notably older, collegiate establishments, tend to make frequent calls on their alumni for donations.

Appeals are often run in conjunction with the Friends group, and this is explored further in section 5.5 below.

Appeals are often launched in conjunction with an application to a funding body where matching funds are required. In these cases, the library or archive would have the added task of putting together an application at the same time as initiating an appeal. If this is going to be the case, it would be advisable to try to combine as much of the initial preparation as possible—there is no point having to go back and do more research which is only slightly different—it is best to do a thorough investigation in the first place.

Appeals are often set up to raise funds for the type of projects which are not covered by the major funding bodies, for example increasing the size of the endowment.

It is important to seek advice from others about setting up an appeal—those who have already been through it are usually only too glad to offer advice if asked politely.

5.2 Adopt-a-Book Schemes

Case study (x)

A variation on the theme of Adopt-a-Book is that in operation at a Learned Society library. Potential donors are asked to sponsor an item in the picture collection, the funds going towards a conservation programme for the collection.

The novelty of this scheme is that it is appealing to those donors who are willing to give quite substantial amounts of money. The donors each receive a high quality photographic print of 'their' picture and a plaque bearing their name is put alongside the original.

The scheme so far has attracted several individual sponsors as well as a company which has sponsored approximately twenty pictures.

Adopt-a-Book schemes often seem to be an add-on to a fundraising initiative rather than forming the initiative in their own right. In its most basic form potential benefactors are invited to give a sum either to purchase a new book or to conserve existing material in the collection. The sum can be enough to pay for a single unit (i.e. a book) or to go into a fund towards the purchase or the required work. The 'reward' for the benefactor, aside from the satisfaction of giving aid, is usually in the form of having a dedication put into the purchased book or being mentioned in reports of the completed conservation work.

Adopt-a-Book schemes usually support the conservation of valuable or significant collection items.

The questionnaire responses show that Adopt-a-Book schemes fall into several categories which are explored below.

5.2.1 Sponsored book purchases

Adopt-a-Book schemes often run alongside other forms of fundraising as a perpetual stream of small donations. University libraries, in particular, seem to have schemes constantly in motion in this way—notably catching the parents of new students and alumni for donations.

5.2.2 Effort involved

Several of the questionnaires which mentioned Adopt-a-Book schemes also mentioned that it took considerable effort to set up and even more to keep the momentum going. One librarian commented:

> The initial response was good but it tailed off after 2 or 3 years. It needed much input from staff to maintain interest in levels of giving and it is debatable whether the income was worth the effort.

The temptation to allow the scheme to drift on without proper effort or indulgence can lead to it becoming a drain on resources rather than an asset.

5.2.3 Advantages

The scheme can encourage donors to give a set amount of money; psychologically this is quite a good tactic and can lead to further donations. It can also be used to show people just how much books cost and therefore to encourage them to think further about the library or archive.

The scheme can increase the donor's feeling of being a stakeholder in the library or archive which may lead to later donations. It can also develop links within an otherwise distant outside world. One Cathedral librarian's comments illustrate this:

> Adopt-a-Book is used to raise funds for the Endowment. Nearly £10,000 has been raised so far. The scheme is especially useful as it gives individuals a link to the library.

Adopt-a-Book allows individuals who can only spare a relatively small amount of money to see exactly where their money is going, rather than feeling that it has disappeared into a huge project where it will make little difference.

5.2.4 Variations on the theme

The Marx Memorial Library have, as part of a large appeal to repair, refurbish and extend their building, schemes called 'buy-a-brick' and 'name-a-shelf' where donors are invited to give £100 (for a brick) or £50 (for a shelf). Again, the benefits of Adopt-a-Book apply—individuals are encouraged to forge a link with the library and can really feel as if their input is making a difference.

5.3 Collection boxes

Collection boxes were generally seen by the respondents of the questionnaires as a useful but relatively insignificant additional source of income. They are generally apparent in archives or libraries where there is no charge for use—such as record offices. Many libraries which do charge for admission also ask for donations but these are often justified by making the donation specific to a certain project or fundraising effort which is underway.

Some libraries and archives which do not directly charge for use of the collection do make a demand for a voluntary contribution which is viewed (unofficially) as compulsory. In these cases, the funds coming from a donations tin or collection box can be quite substantial and form part of the anticipated core revenue generation.

The way in which a donations box is displayed can markedly effect its capacity to generate income. As an example, one questionnaire respondent mentioned that since they repositioned their box to make it more prominent and put a large well-produced notice over it stating the need for donations and suggesting the amount of one pound each, donations have increased markedly from the previous average of thirty pence each. There is no element of compulsion, but by bringing the need for donations to the attention of the visitor this change has given an increase in revenue from the donations box of approximately two hundred pounds per week.

5.4 Sponsorship

Case study (xi)

Birmingham Libraries

At Birmingham Central Library an interesting idea which unfortunately did not come to fruition was the idea of selling advertising space on borrowers' cards. The main reason that the scheme was not carried out was a lack of successful approaches to sponsors— the approaches were made by the central sponsorship officer and it was thought, in hindsight, that this may have been something that would have been better carried out by library staff. The main advantages of this sponsorship would be that it would provide a net contribution to the running of the library.

Another possibility arising from this was the idea of advertising on date labels—these have to be produced as part of the day-to-day running of the library and to get a sponsor to cover the printing costs would be a great advantage. However, there was concern about how long the labels would be around before they were used—if the sponsor changed their details or went out of business during this period the labels would have to be discarded.

The idea of receiving money towards costs in return for a bit of publicity for the benefactor is an attractive prospect and the library and archive community certainly seem to be trying to make the most of the sponsorship available. Individuals, businesses and Friends groups are the most likely sponsors.

5.4.1 What is sponsored?

Publications

The questionnaires suggested that sponsorship was sought most frequently for publications. Often this took the form of the sponsor paying the publication costs in return for some publicity within the text. The types of businesses who will sponsor publications are often related in some way to the content of the work or the book trade. For example:

Our *Special Collections Guide* was sponsored by a local bookshop and by an architectural and design firm.

An interesting comment was made by the archivist of a local studies archive. They had sought sponsorship for their 1994/95 Annual Report and had subsequently been able to publish in 'glossy' format. This is an example of sponsorship enabling the existing service to be upgraded and allowing a more elegant publication to be produced.

Mailings and publicity material

Sponsors are often sought for publicity material such as posters and leaflets. The benefit to the sponsor from this is that their name will be seen by a wide range of people. The questionnaires suggested that this type of sponsorship did not involve large amounts of money but was a useful way to offset costs.

Food and drink at an event

Sponsors are often sought to provide refreshments for events such as book launches. Again, this is a way of offsetting the cost of an event which is not a 'core' cost.

5.4.2 The benefits of sponsorship

The benefits of sponsorship need not be primarily financial. There are benefits in terms of contacts developed and publicity received. It can be seen as a way of raising the profile of the institution or event without spending directly on publicity.

5.4.3 What does the sponsor expect in return?

The questionnaire responses suggested that sponsorship was, unsurprisingly, largely dependent on the sponsor receiving something in return. Usually this takes the form of the company name being made visible before a range of potential customers. This unfortunately means that it is often only high-profile projects which attract sponsorship. One comment was that the amount of sponsorship available was dependent on the potential press interest. Another comment was that when seeking sponsorship for a publication they found that local branches of national businesses would expect members of the royal family to be involved before they could offer any financial assistance. It seems that local businesses are more likely than branches of national businesses to help local causes.

It is important carefully to explore the areas of interest of the company or person and to show that they are being approached because of this, not because they are on a long list of several potential sponsors who are all receiving the same blanket approaches (even if this is the case). As with all other areas of revenue generation, research has to be undertaken if the approach is to be successful.

5.4.4 Disadvantages

The general feeling is that seeking sponsorship is hard work, and often a fruitless occupation. Some libraries and archives which are part of a larger institution have the benefit of using the central sponsorship officer; however, this has its problems if the item or event to be sponsored is somewhat specialised. There is a need to liaise and work closely together.

There were also some expressions of embarrassment about seeking sponsorship. This was particularly true of local government funded libraries and archives who were asking the business community for sponsorship—businesses often feel that they have contributed enough through taxes.

In conclusion, sponsorship can be a useful way of offsetting costs, particularly those which arise from special events or projects. However, as with other sources of funds, seeking sponsorship has become competitive. Potential sponsors are demanding more in return for their investment and making their recipients work harder for it.

5.5 Friends

Case study (xii)

The Friends of Hackney Archives

Hackney Archives lay claim to setting up the first Friends group for a London Borough Record Office; the Friends of Hackney Archives were set up in 1985. There were two main reasons for setting up the group: firstly, to provide a user group who could be called upon to represent the views of the users of the archives; and secondly as a local history society they would provide a marketing framework for publications and materials.

Subscription costs £6 a year, £4.50 of which covers the cost of four newsletters a year and an annual publication. This publication, Hackney History, *costs £3 to non-members. The group currently has over 180 members, and is 'ticking over'. Most of the current members are primarily interested in receiving the news, publications and offers which they are kept informed about through the newsletters. A lot of work goes into the Friends—the staff of Hackney Archives produce the four newsletters each year. However, the large annual publication is produced entirely by the chair of the Friends group.*

The FHA, as with most Friends groups, maintains a small donations fund. This was used as a war chest for the archives during the most severe budget cuts of the late 1980s, moreover the Friends also organised protests against these cuts. They assist with purchases and contribute to projects including document purchases and conservation costs. They have also assisted with buying a computer, but this needed to be justified by being part of a project to improve the Friends' membership database.

Many of the members are not local people—they are often people who have moved away from the area but want to keep up with events. Partly because of this, and also because there is an element of competition for members with another local history group, the group does not have regular meetings. The group has an Annual General Meeting, a well-attended annual lecture (usually sixty to seventy people attend), occasional local walks and infrequent meetings.

It is a good public relations exercise for the Council to have this group—it is very useful to have a defined user group who can be fed with certain issues. They can also act as a consultative body; for example, FHA were consulted when a new computer system was needed for the search room.

This is a real example of the Friends working together with an archive to achieve a situation which is of benefit to both parties.

Case study (xiii)

The Friends Group was established for the following reasons: the then Librarian was very keen, and had considerable experience from his earlier posts; and the Library was very short of money having been badly hit by the financial cuts of the early 1980s, and there was literally nothing for anything other than basic services. It was hoped that the Friends would act to raise much needed extra funds.

The philosophy behind the Friends (at least initially) was that its purpose should be purely to help the Library to raise funds to support non-core activities, which in practice (but not always) usually meant archives and special collections. In this it was relatively successful in its early years, and valuable contributions were made towards the purchase of other manuscript collections, rare titles, and equipment which otherwise would not have been bought. The Friends were also an asset in providing a network of potential contacts—people who could be asked to help (usually financially) if needed, or who could provide links to others in a similar position. The vast majority of members usually had some existing or previous connection with either the Library or the University, the largest group being retired members of staff.

In recent years, unfortunately, membership has dwindled, and the Friends appear to have become more of a social club than a fundraising group. On the whole, more time now appears to be spent by the Library in support of the Friends than vice versa.

The advice given by the librarian who provided case study (xiii) is:

> Anyone setting up a Friends group should make sure from the very start that prospective members (especially Committee members) understand the purpose of the Group, and that fundraising should be fully and properly costed.

Many libraries and archives have a Friends organisation—a group of interested individuals who support the work of the institution in various ways. They may act as a fundraising arm or as a source of voluntary work and specialist knowledge. Groups can even be international—several well known libraries and archives have American Friends who can prove to be a very useful source of funds.

The responses to our questionnaire indicate that, as with most schemes, there are both benefits and disadvantages to be gained from running a Friends scheme. The advantages include:

- Access to a group of people who will raise funds for projects and purchases;

- A source of income from subscriptions;

- A potential vehicle for publicity;

- A pool of skills and expertise which can be called upon when needed;

- The potential to use them as volunteer workers;

- Having at hand a group which could qualify as a partner in funding applications.

The disadvantages noted in the questionnaire responses include:

- Friends groups can take up a lot of staff time;

- In some cases the subscriptions barely cover the cost of running the group;

- The group might disagree with the library or archive over the funding of projects.

5.5.1 Fundraising

The widest use made of Friends seems to be as the fundraising arm of the library or archive. In the questionnaires a common remark was that fundraising, particularly through applying to grant-giving bodies, is such a time-consuming exercise that paid staff simply do not have the time to do it. Having a group on hand who are able to take on at least some of this work would seem the ideal solution.

The fundraising efforts of Friends groups can take several directions. On a simple level, the money provided by their subscriptions can be a useful resource. The archivist in the case study (ix), above, recounts how the formation of their Friends groups coincided with a desperate appeal to raise enough money for a purchase which was due to come up at auction. The high profile nature of the appeal provided publicity for the new group and the resulting subscriptions provided more than enough money for the purchase.

Friends groups can also co-ordinate appeals and provide the grass roots level research and leg work needed for such projects. Their value as a volunteer labour force in this sense is that they are generally more experienced and responsible than a regular 'volunteer'. They are also, by their very nature, expected to be interested in the upkeep of the institution and so may introduce extra passion in the search for necessary funds. However, some libraries and archives made the comment that while they welcomed the income from subscriptions and from the occasional legacy or donation they would not seek to involve the Friends further in fundraising because of the extra work this would place on the paid staff.

If the Friends are given sole responsibility for fundraising then it may be acceptable that staff time is invested in them. Fundraising has become, in a sense, a core activity and should receive its share of investment.

Another use of the Friends as a source of funds was where they were seen as a type of 'rainy day' fund which would not be used except on certain purchases or as an emergency fund. Case study (xii) illustrates how Hackney Archives relied on their Friends for emergency funds during a particularly hard spending freeze in the 1980s.

An interesting attitude from some quarters was that it would be unfair to ask Friends to contribute to fundraising given that they already gave support through their subscriptions. A leading independent library said that they would not establish a Friends group with the purpose of asking them to raise funds as this would be akin to an abuse of their generosity. The aim of having them would be that they would be able to work with the library. Others had a less altruistic outlook and saw their Friends as a resource to utilise whenever necessary.

Where a Friends group is large enough to provide substantial sums of money they can be a useful partner for grant applications.

5.5.2 General support

Friends are also seen as a general support unit—a group of people who are going to support the library or archive against the rest of the world. In most cases they are genuinely 'friends' of the organisation. One charming example comes from a cathedral library where 'a small group of "pious women" collect loose coppers and provide £50 to £60 a year'. The sums may not be large but having a group of genuinely interested people to hand is worth much more than the money alone.

5.5.3 Volunteer workers

The membership of Friends groups often consists largely of retired professionals and former staff members and this provides a useful source of advice and expertise for the institution. One questionnaire mentioned practical help received on an archive indexing project and an illustrations database project. Aside from sparing the cost of a hired professional the advice given is more likely to be relevant to the organisation.

5.5.4 Problems

The most frequent complaint about Friends groups which came out of the questionnaires was that they took up more of the paid staff's time than their contribution warranted. In short, they created work rather than money. It seems that the administration of the scheme often falls to the library or archive and is inhibiting to the further development of its potential benefits. Friends, evidently, are seen as a success mostly where they were run independently and require minimal input from the institution. However, it could be argued that a good Friends group would be worth investing time in as they have the potential to be a great asset.

A variation on this was the comment that often the library or archive ends up financially supporting the Friends, rather than the other way around. A number of questionnaires even said that they had disbanded their Friends after making the discovery that they were subsidising their activities. A general feeling seemed to be that the Friends needed constant regeneration if they were to remain of use to the organisation.

Although it is seen as preferable for the Friends group to run itself, and thus make less call on the resources of the library or archive, this brings new problems with it. The parent organisation no longer has control over the group and thus can lose the right to determine how the Friends spend their funds.

5.5.5 Conflicts arising within institutions

A common complaint made in the questionnaires was that the library or archive would like to set up a Friends group but could not because of conflicts within the parent organisation. This was particularly the case in cathedral libraries and archives where they were unable to form their own Friends group because of an existing Friends of the Cathedral. The problems developed where they got no real help from this group. This situation was also apparent in some museum libraries. In the case of cathedrals the problems were not confined to the establishment of Friends groups—there was a general problem with raising funds as the needs of the fabric of the cathedral were usually seen as a higher priority than the needs of the library or archive.

5.5.6 Similar schemes

Where it is not appropriate to have a Friends group there are other options. One learned society library has a membership scheme which worked in a similar way. Other libraries and archives recognise their volunteer workers as their Friends. In record offices where Family History societies are active they often develop into quasi-Friends.

In conclusion, having a Friends group can be a real bonus: they can support the library or archive in all manner of situations; they can help to finance initiatives; and they can be a useful source of expert advice. It is, however, important to ensure that their role is kept in balance with the input made by the library or archive; if they become a draw on resources then their role needs to be re-evaluated.

5.6 Marketing

Case study (xiv)

Birmingham Libraries

Conflict occurred when Birmingham Central Library was operating a small shop selling library related materials such as books and postcards. The chair of the small business council in the town was concerned about the potential effect on local trade and she reminded the library that to run a commercial enterprise in this way was ultra vires—*the Libraries and Museums Act 1964 restricts charging for goods and services. The library would therefore only be allowed to sell items which it produces itself such as books and postcards—it cannot market commercially published books or other outsourced products.*

This act does not relate to record offices and so many of these do successfully run book- and souvenir shops.

The extent to which libraries and archives can raise revenue through direct marketing of products and services depends on several factors, notably:

- Do you have something to sell?

- Do you have somewhere to sell it?

- Do you have adequate staff resources to implement it?

- What do you hope to get in return?

There is also the need to assess the potential profit to input ratio of the exercise. For example, one archive mentioned that while its marketing of publications and postcards was 'mildly successful' in that it earned £4000 per year this was insignificant compared to the £30,000 per year income from grants from owners of manuscripts.

Unfortunately, there is an increasing need for libraries and archives to develop their fundraising in this area because of a lack of core funding. Increasingly, institutions are bound by contract to raise a certain amount of their income through the sale of goods and services. One librarian mentioned that this proportion was as high as 30 per cent for his library.

It is important to ask for legal advice when contemplating raising revenue from marketing. Tax is payable on anything above 'incidental trading'. In assessing what tax is payable the Inland Revenue take into consideration the objects of the organisation. If the items sold are directly linked to this aim, e.g. for the purposes of education, they are exempt. Therefore a museum may not have to pay tax on its sale of books but would have to do so on postcards, slides, mugs and so on—they are not regarded as educational and are therefore not exempt. If the non-educational sales exceed 20% of the total turnover tax is payable on all sales. In such circumstances it may be beneficial to form a trading company, but take the advice of an accountant on this. If the organisation is government funded it is difficult to set up a trading company.

5.6.1 The need for an outlet

A major consideration for any library or archive seeking to sell any items is the need to find somewhere, and someone, to sell them. Any potential profit could be wiped out by the staff time needed to take payments and organise stock. Space itself is often at a premium in smaller libraries and archives. All the factors need to be carefully weighed up. Even the idea of selling postcards at the issue desk or other staffed outlet may cause problems, an Oxbridge college noted:

> The college has investigated the possibility of postcards in the past but it found that it did not pay as the only sales outlet is the lodge and lodge staff are too busy to promote sales actively.

This is an extreme example—most places probably do not have to deal with fractious students while trying to count out postcards for tourists—but it illustrates the point that all factors need to be taken into consideration.

5.6.2 The importance of effective marketing

A frequent comment made about selling items was that even if products were initially well thought out and costed efficiently they failed to sell as well as expected because they were not marketed to their best advantage. A simple response to this could be that the skills of information professionals cannot reasonably be expected to extend to those of business. Therefore in some ways these ventures may be doomed to fail unless money is spent on expert advice—which is often not a realistic possibility. It seems that to make the leap from selling a few books and postcards at the issue desk to running a trading outlet often requires more effort and money than the library or archive can afford to invest.

If an outside agency can be persuaded to take over the marketing of a product then the benefits to the library or archive can often be increased. Several questionnaires mentioned that they handed over the marketing and publicity of their publications to professionals and were pleased to pass on this responsibility. However, this is more likely to be possible in larger, more high profile institutions such as national museums and libraries.

5.6.3 Items that are frequently marketed

Postcards

The ubiquitous postcard was an important topic of discussion in the responses to the questionnaire. It seems that almost all of the libraries and archives who responded to the questionnaire had postcards for sale to their customers and yet the comments made were generally negative. Possibly the most frequent comment was that postcards do not really raise a lot of money but are seen to be good public relations tools. The initial outlay is also seen as prohibitive, partly because of the slow return on the initial investment.

As an example, the cost of the original transparency for each design of postcard would be around £40 and then there would be some further costs involved in the checking of proofs and so on. The standard cost of each card may be as low as five to ten pence, if the order is in the region of five thousand copies. It can be seen, therefore, that if you are able to order in large enough quantities the return can be substantial; as much as twenty five pence on each card if you sell them for thirty pence each. However, this is only if you are able to order a large quantity—if you do not have the capital to spend on a large order the margin and the returns will be less. There is also the need to take the costs of storing the cards if a large order is placed, and the idea that it may well be some time before the cost is recouped.

It could be argued that if a postcard has the apparently hidden benefit of being an 'aide-memoire' and of acting as publicity as well as making money then it is perhaps not that much of a problem if sales only just cover costs—as long as costs are rigorously worked out and are the true costs (i.e. including staff time, storage, etc.).

Publications

One of the most frequently mentioned items for sale were publications which have a strong link to the library or archive—usually they have been produced in-house (particularly by record offices) or they are thematically linked (concerning the local area or a particular part of the collection). A frequent comment was that the sale of such publications may not necessarily make much of a profit but that they serve to raise the profile of the library or archive within the community and strengthen their claim to being a valuable community resource. The following is a comment from a local studies archive:

> We sell local history publications which we have produced (as well as other people's), e.g. town trails, postcards, brief histories. Their effect is to raise our profile rather than to generate income; if we costed staff time they would make a loss.

The comment about the large cost of staff input into producing publications is mentioned in several questionnaire responses but this is not generally seen as much of a problem—the need to disseminate information and develop links with the community is seen to outweigh costs.

Reprints or facsimiles of material in the collection are also frequently produced for sale.

Other items

Other items mentioned in the questionnaires included replicas of art objects in the collection, Christmas cards and prints from pictures.

One learned society archive had produced replicas of scientific instruments in the collection but had found they were too highly priced to sell well. The market for objects must be thoroughly researched.

An interesting argument in one response was that they had resisted producing facsimiles or replicas of items in the collection for fear that this would de-value the original articles. It is hard to see how this can be so when other questionnaire responses extolled the virtues of marketing replicas as a way to publicise the collections.

Christmas cards are also a good vehicle for publicity, if not notably for profit. The librarian of one library which produces Christmas cards notes that while the profit is not large, the cards help to convey the message that they are a charity. She also remarks that the Christmas card market is increasingly competitive and should be entered with extreme care. Unlike postcards, Christmas cards are often marketed widely through mailshots and so can reach a whole new audience. However, this type of publicity is not cheap.

Selling items donated for the purpose

Membership libraries, in particular, can raise some unearned income through the sale of books donated by members for sale.

One membership library has an annual 'bring and buy' book sale: members bring in unwanted books/journals and the library has first choice to fill gaps in their holdings. The remainder is offered for sale to members and their friends at very reasonable prices; this usually yields around £200—£300 to library funds annually. Any books that are unsold are put in the cloakroom area for interested parties to help themselves from—this raises about £10 a week which goes into the petty cash.

5.6.4 Reproduction fees

Reproduction fees featured regularly in the questionnaire responses, but the attitude towards them varied somewhat. There was a marked distinction between those who charged cost price for the service and those who ran it as a revenue generating enterprise. This depended largely on whether it was viewed as an extra service or as part of the core provision, and also on the type of customer using the service.

> Reproduction fees are very productive. I regret that other record offices are too often willing to waive fees, even for commercial publishers. No firm market can therefore be established.

Unfortunately not all libraries or archives have the facilities to run a reprint programme and the comment below is all too familiar:

> Occasional sales are made of copy photographs and handling charges are made for publication of photographs, but the service is underfunded and understaffed and there is no time for promotion.

Again, it is the common story of needing extra money and staff resources to develop a revenue-generating service. However, it could be argued that providing a reprint or photography service also has a conservation purpose—the photography cost of an item which has not previously been photographed can be borne by the customer, the negative is then placed in the archive and all subsequent requests for copies are taken from it.

However, setting up a reproduction service has its drawbacks. Customers can come to expect more than the library or archive wants to give:

> We eventually managed to resist an Australian researcher who wanted us to consent to and supervise the microfilming of much of our Nineteenth Century pamphlet collection for their Library—merely for the cost of the microfilming. I think the refusal was reasonable as it is a unique collection.

This comment shows that the liquid boundaries of such services are open to misinterpretation and even abuse.

The issues of ownership and copyright can also cause problems. The archive or library **must** be careful to retain copyright when allowing outside agencies to produce reproductions from originals—seek legal advice.

The development of new formats is also creating changes in the nature of reproduction provision. Several questionnaires mentioned the provision of images for commercially produced CD-ROMs and video. The digital media are generally causing a few problems in the library and archive community—electronic publishers can provide full colour images more cheaply and in greater numbers than they could in print and so the pressure is on the image providers to keep up with their pace. One comment encapsulates this perfectly:

> Problems are caused by the increasing number of requests for high-volume reproduction of unique material received from image-hungry commercial

digitisation enterprises; it is our experience that such customers are often reluctant to pay unit fees comparable to the long-accepted practice in respect of reproductions to be made in more traditional media, while we ourselves are reluctant to charge much less for use in one media than in another.

It seems that this is an area where a united approach needs to be developed; there is the potential for a huge amount of work to be created without the corresponding rise in revenue.

One area that seems to be growing to the benefit of archives and libraries is the production of CD-ROMs about local history for schools. Whereas previously locally-published teaching materials were small-scale, the advent of CD-ROM means that better quality material can be produced relatively cheaply and easily. Although it is debatable about how much revenue could be generated in this way (possibly between two departments of the same council) it is a way to develop a relationship with the community and should have long-term benefits. One record office gave the figure of £3000 as their income from collaboration on a CD-ROM.

CD-ROM also offers new marketing potential for images—the most popular, or well used, images could be bundled together on a mass-produced CD and sold. This could well cut down the staff time spent on individual image requests.

Another source of income is royalty payments and although the area is too vast to go into much detail a scheme which many librarians and archivists mentioned is the National Inventory of Documentary Sources (NIDS), a microfilm publication published by Chadwyck-Healey. The publication is made up of listings of the contents of collections prepared by the librarian or archivist—the publisher buys the rights to film and distribute these lists or catalogues and the institution receives royalty payments in return.[23]

5.6.5 Renting out premises

Renting out buildings for private use and functions can be a good way of generating revenue, and it also has the advantage that this revenue will be earned out of the usual opening hours and therefore will not impinge on the normal functioning of the library or archive. However, this relies heavily on the suitability of the premises, the facilities available and countless other considerations such as available car parking and alcohol licences. By bringing people onto the premises you will of course in any case be raising awareness of the institution and its significance in the wider community.

Unfortunately, this is another revenue-generating idea that will require an investment of time and money to make it viable. Nevertheless, if the premises are noteworthy in terms of their architecture or location there could be some mileage in investigating the possibilities. Even having an attractive garden can be a potential selling point for a function. The recent changes in the laws surrounding marriage could also have potential for picturesque or historical premises.

---

[23] Enquiries about NIDS should be sent to Chadwyck-Healey Ltd; Cambridge Place, Cambridge CB2 1NR.

As well as providing the premises for a function there could be some benefits in providing other services for them. One well known library installed a light refreshments facility—this not only earns £5000 per year but also makes the premises more attractive for people seeking a venue. In this capacity it has created a £3000 per year increase in facility fees.

5.6.6 The marketing of staff skills

One of the comments which was repeated in several questionnaires was the need for the profession to be more aware of the value of its expertise and knowledge. There was a general feeling that if concerted effort was made to raise the profile of librarians and archivists revenue could result—for example, revenue, from consultancy and advice, rather than giving these for free. The archivist of one local government record office commented:

> I insist on being paid and encourage publishers to think of us commercially. In general, I am more interested in selling expertise rather than objects. The specialist skills we have in our midst are extremely marketable.

However, there is a danger in this approach—by demanding payment for services which had previously been free there is the likelihood that others will follow suit. For example, sources of free advice used by libraries and archives could dry up—leading to an overall gain of zero.

Distinction also needs to be made between the customers of an archive or library—it may well be acceptable to charge a publishing company for advice but the work of ordinary researchers or students would be severely impeded by such actions.

5.7 Charging for Access and Value-Added Services

Case study (xv)

Hackney Archives—Record Agent

This began at Hackney when staff levels fell too low to cope with sustaining a search service. Tenders were invited for a record agent and the contract was duly given out. The Archives organised all the stationery and a leaflet for customers explaining the service and the standard of work they could expect. The Record Agent works in Hackney Archives for at least one day a week. The service costs £12 per hour (in half hour blocks) and the customer is billed by London Borough of Hackney Trading; the Record Agent is then paid from this after LBHT has taken a reasonable cut.

The service works well because the Record Agent is self-employed and thus Hackney Archives have no employer responsibilities or costs. The Agent is dedicated to this service and the archives guarantee the level of service which the customer can expect.

It seems that many types of value-added services are now charged for in most libraries and archives. In some cases charges are also levied for basic access to the collections. The questionnaire responses suggested that the types of services which were revenue generating were standard throughout the community.

5.7.1 Access charges

Where it is feasible, and where no constitutional clauses prevent it, many libraries and archives charge fees for using the collections. It does, naturally, depend largely on the type of institution and its users—it would not be perceived as acceptable for a record office or a public library to charge the Community Charge paying public to use its collections.

There is usually a scale of charges depending on the type of user—for example, universities often charge external users to use their library but the fee is usually less, or waived, if they are alumni or current students of another university. Fees are often scaled as regards the users' rights as well—borrowing is more expensive than consulting items in-house. In some cases visits are limited to a certain number or limited to certain times of the day. One university librarian said that these fees were a more important source of day-to-day funds than any other scheme.

Charging for access has the added benefit of making the collection seem more valuable and somehow more exclusive. Requiring readers also to produce references has a similar effect.

Problems with charging for access can develop where the library is part of a larger institution—for example, in a cathedral. One cathedral librarian said that their desire to implement a realistic charge for what amounted to an hour-long tour of the library with full commentary was made difficult by the fact that access to the archives of the same cathedral cost only 25 pence.

If the people requesting access to the library or archive are there as tourists rather than to consult the material for an academic purpose it seems that a charge is generally levied. One librarian commented that as well as raising large sums of money through guided tours there were added bonuses within the institution:

> Tours raise interest in the Library as a 'heritage' resource among members of the parent body. The resulting praise is good for staff morale and helps to present a friendly public image.

5.7.2 Income raised through charging for photocopying

Somewhat surprisingly, the humble photocopier has become a major revenue earner for libraries and archives. Many of the questionnaire responses mentioned it as a key source of income.

5.7.3 Charging for a research service

Charging for research has become commonplace, particularly in record offices and local studies centres. There are frequently not enough staff to deal with detailed enquiries as part of their normal working hours. Moreover, users of most libraries and archives are expected to do their own research using the material in the collection.

Charging for the service often only covers the cost of the time spent on the enquiry but even so this charge will encourage customers to focus their requests. One record office was quite blatant in their use of charging for this service—it 'helps to reduce the workload'.

Research services can also be developed more thoroughly, if there is a need, as in the case of Hackney Archives in case study (xv) above.

5.8 Payment-in-kind

Payment-in-kind is something of a grey area for libraries and archives and often takes the form of providing a service for a reduced cost, or free, in return for some form of non-monetary payment at a later date. The most spectacular example in the responses was the redundant church which was given to a county record office by the diocese in exchange for work carried out on diocesan archives.

5.8.1 Books received in lieu of reproduction fee

This is the major area of payment-in-kind mentioned in the responses to the questionnaires. This is useful for the library or archive because it can add a useful publication to the collection or the item can be sold. Arrangements such as these usually occur when the publication is being produced by another public body or by an academic or educational source. Commercial publishers are rarely granted such concessions! However, one record office has a scheme in operation which deals with both groups of customers:

> Reproduction fees for items to be reproduced in books are waived in return for copies of the book (private authors), or in return for free copies of the book for resale in the office (commercial publishers).

The new technologies are also providing a source for this kind of payment—one private library received a highly priced CD-ROM in return for allowing collection material to be put into the database. This had the double benefit of providing a free resource for readers to use but also the processing that had been performed on the collection material would otherwise not have been carried out. However, this did rather assume that the library had the necessary computer equipment to use the CD.

5.8.2 Review copies of books

Offering to review new publications can often lead to review copies worth hundreds of pounds being added to stock. However, this rather depends on having suitable experts on staff to undertake the reviewing.

5.8.3 Results of research presented as payment for access to collections

Many record offices mentioned that they often received copies of the work of Family History Societies, usually on microfilm. This is also often the case when the Mormons are using the collection for their research.

6 APPENDICES

6.1 Libraries and Archives Contributing to This Report

The authors would like to extend very many thanks to the librarians and archivists who spared their time to complete the questionnaires; these responses were a vital part of the research for this report.

- Armagh Public (Robinson) Library
- The Athenaeum Library
- The Bank of England Archive
- Bath and North East Somerset Record Office
- Bath Royal Literary and Scientific Institution
- Bedford Central Library, Local Studies Library
- Bedfordshire County Record Office
- Birmingham City Archives
- Bradford Libraries
- Brasenose College Archives, Oxford
- Bristol Record Office
- British Architectural Library
- British Architectural Library, Drawings Collection
- British Library of Political and Economic Science
- British Telecom Archives
- Buckinghamshire Record Office
- Canterbury Cathedral Archives
- Carlisle Cathedral Library
- Chelmsford Cathedral Library
- Cheshire County Council Archives and Local Studies
- Chester Cathedral Library
- Chetham's Library
- Chichester Cathedral Library
- Christ Church Library, Oxford
- Cornwall County Record Office
- Cumbria County Record Offices
- Devon and Exeter Institution Library
- Dorset County Archives Service
- Essex Record Office
- Exeter Cathedral Library
- Exeter University Library
- Folkestone Heritage Collection
- GlaxoWellcome
- Gloucestershire Record Office
- Greater Manchester County Record Office
- Guildhall Library Manuscripts Section
- Guinness Archives and Records Centre
- Hackney Archives Department
- Hammersmith and Fulham Archives and Local History Centre
- Hampshire Record Office
- Hatfield House Library
- Hereford Cathedral Library
- Hertfordshire Record Office
- House of Lords Record Office
- Hudson Memorial Library, Cathedral and Abbey Church of St Alban
- Imperial College Archives
- Imperial War Museum, Department of Printed Books
- Innerpeffray Library
- The International Heritage Centre
- Ipswich Institute Reading Room and Library
- Ironbridge Gorge Museum, Library and Archives
- King's College London Archives and Liddell Hart Centre for Military Archives
- Lambeth Palace Library
- Lancashire Record Office
- The Leeds Library
- Leicestershire Record Office
- Lewisham Local Studies and Archives
- The Library of the Guildford Institute of the University of Surrey
- Library of the College of Royal Physicians of Edinburgh
- Library of the Linnean Society of London
- Library of the Religious Society of Friends in Britain
- Lichfield Cathedral Library
- Lincoln Cathedral Library
- Lincolnshire Archives
- Linen Hall Library, Belfast
- London Borough of Enfield, Records Management
- The London Library
- London Metropolitan Archives
- The Marx Memorial Library
- Marylebone Cricket Club Library, Museum and Archives
- The Mass-Observation Archive, University of Sussex Library
- Mercers' Company Archive
- Merton College Library, Oxford
- National Maritime Museum Library
- Natural History Museum Library
- New College Archives, Oxford,
- New Hall Cambridge, Rosemary Murray Library
- Norfolk County Record Office
- Northamptonshire Record Office
- Norwich Cathedral, Dean and Chapter Library
- Nottingham Subscription Library
- Nottinghamshire Archives

- Oriel College Archives, Oxford
- Oxfordshire Archives
- Oxfordshire Health Authority Archives
- The Portico Library, London
- Queen's College Library, Cambridge
- Rochester Cathedral Library
- Rochester-upon-Medway Studies Centre
- Royal Botanic Garden Edinburgh
- Royal College of Veterinary Surgeons, Wellcome Library
- Royal Entomological Society Library
- Royal Geographical Society Archives
- Royal Geographical Society Library
- Royal Institute of International Affairs Library
- Royal Opera House Archives
- Royal Society Library
- RSA Library and Archive
- Salisbury Cathedral Library
- Sheffield Archives
- Society of Antiquaries of London Library
- Somerville College Library, Oxford
- St Alban's Cathedral Muniment Room
- St Andrew's Cathedral Library, Inverness
- St Columb's Cathedral, Chapter House Library
- St Edmund Hall Library, Oxford
- St George's Chapel Archives and Chapter Library, Windsor Castle
- St John's College Library, Cambridge
- St Patrick's College, Maynooth : John Paul II Library and Russell Library
- St Paul's Cathedral Library
- Suffolk Record Office
- Surrey Record Office
- Tate Gallery Archive
- Tyne and Wear Archives Service
- University College London Library
- University of Bristol Theatre Collection
- University of Hull, Brynmor Jones Library
- University of Leeds Library
- University of Liverpool, Sydney Jones Library
- University of London Library
- University of Newcastle, Robinson Library
- University of Nottingham Library, Department of Manuscripts and Special Collections
- University of Southampton, Hartley Library
- University of Sussex Library
- University of Wales, Cardiff Library
- University of Wales, Swansea Library
- University of Westminster Archive
- West Sussex Record Office
- Westerkirk Library
- William Salt Library
- Wiltshire Record Office
- Wolverhampton Archives and Local Studies
- York Minster Library
- The Zoological Society of London

6.2 The Questionnaire

This questionnaire was sent to approximately 500 libraries and archives in the UK and Ireland.

1. Please state the name of your library or archive.

e.g. British Architectural Library
    Hereford Cathedral Library
    Herts County Record Office

1.1. How would you categorise your institution?

e.g. County record office.

2. If it is part of a larger organisation or is dependent on another body, please give brief details.

e.g. Royal Institute of British Architects.
    Herts County Council.

2.1. Does the larger organisation provide you with full funding? If not how is the shortfall made up?

e.g. Membership schemes.

3. Please give your name, function and contact details.

4. Please state briefly what kinds of additional fundraising your library or archive has used—and your experience of them:

4.1. Grants from External Funding Bodies (including the Lottery) [yes/no]

If yes, which bodies have you approached. What has been your experience?

4.2. Appeals [yes/no]

If yes, were they general (i.e. public campaigns) or targeted (i.e. *Adopt-A-Book*)? What has been your experience?

4.3. 'Friends' schemes [yes/no]

What has been your experience?

4.4. Marketing based on collection items [yes/no]

What has been your experience?

4.5. Sponsorship, e.g. of specific events or publications [yes/no] e.g. providing drinks for promotional events. What has been your experience?

4.6. Indirect sources of support/ non-monetary contributions [yes/no]

e.g. volunteers, collaborative cataloguing projects.

5. Do you have any other comments or remarks which you feel would be valuable to share?

e.g. why did you choose to pursue funding in this way?

6.3 Useful Addresses

Please note that addresses for the funding agencies which are described in this *Guide* can be found in Section 3.3.

ASLIB
Information House
20-24 Old Street
London EC1V 9AP
Tel: 0171-253 4488

The Association of Independent Libraries
c/o Geoffrey Forster
The Leeds Library
18, Commercial Street
Leeds LS1 6AL
Tel: 0113-245 3071

The Association of Independent Museums
c/o Sam Mullins
London Transport Museum
Covent Garden
London WC2E 7BB

The Cathedral Libraries and Archives Association
The Secretary (Ms D Mortimer)
York Minster Library
Deans Park
York YO1 2JD
Tel: 01904-625 308

Charities Aid Foundation
48 Pembury Road
Tonbridge
Kent TN9 2JD
Tel: 01732-520 000

The Department of National Heritage
2-4 Cockspur Street
London SW1Y 5DH
Tel: 0171-211 6200

The Directory of Social Change
24 Stephenson Way
London NW1 2DP
Tel: 0171-209 5151

The Federation of Family History Societies
The Benson Room
Birmingham and Midland Institution
Margaret Street
Birmingham B3 3BS

The Historic Libraries Forum
c/o Peter Hingley
Librarian
Royal Astronomical Society
Burlington House
Piccadilly
London W1V ONL
Email: pdh@ras.org.uk

The Library and Information Commission
The British Library
2 Sheraton Street
London W1V 4BH
Email: LIC@bl.uk

The Library Association
7 Ridgmount Street
London WC1E 7AE
Tel: 0171-636 7543

London Learned Societies Libraries
c/o Peter Hingley
Librarian
Royal Astronomical Society
Burlington House
Piccadilly
London W1V ONL
Email: pdh@ras.org.uk

Museums and Galleries Commission
16 Queen Anne's Gate
London SW1H 9AA
Tel: 0171-233 4200

The Museums Association
42 Clerkenwell Close
London EC1R 0AU
Tel: 0171-608 2933

The National Council on Archives
c/o Nicholas Kingsley
Birmingham City Archives
Central Library
Chamberlain Square
Birmingham B3 3HQ

National Preservation Office
Great Russell Street
London WC1B 3DG
Tel: 0171-412 7612
Email: NPO@bl.uk

NADFAS
NADFAS House
8 Guilford Street
London WC1N 1DT
Tel: 0171-430 0730

The Royal Commission on Historical Manuscripts
Quality House
Quality Court
Chancery Lane
London WC2A 1HP
Tel: 0171-242 1198

The Society of Archivists
Information House
20-24 Old Street
London EC1V 9AP
Tel: 0171-253 5087

6.4 Useful Internet Sites

The Royal Commission on Historical Manuscripts: **http://www.hmc.gov.uk/**

The British Library Research and Innovation Centre: **http://portico.bl.uk/ric/**
How to apply for a BL RIC Grant: **http://portico.bl.uk/ric/toapply/overview.html**

The Department of National Heritage: **http://www.heritage.gov.uk/index.html**

Mailbase—for details of UK based email discussion lists: **http://mailbase.ac.uk/**
Lis-Libhist. This email discussion list covers matters relating to library history and historic libraries. For more information, see the Mailbase site:
http://www.mailbase.ac.uk/lists/lis-libhist/

UK Fundraising: a resource for UK charity and nonprofit fundraisers. This site covers such topics as: books/reviews; courses; events (seminars, training sessions, etc.) for fundraisers; examples of online fundraising; grants and funding; information and resources (UK and international); magazines; nonprofit resources (UK and international); products, services, advisers (UK): **http://www.fundraising.co.uk/**

6.5 Select Bibliography

Directories, etc.

Applying for Grant Aid: Advice to Custodians, Advisory Memorandum No 3, London: The Royal Commission on Historical Manuscripts, 1993

The Arts Funding Guide, 1994/5 edition, Anne-Marie Doulton, London: Directory of Social Change

The Directory of Grant Making Trusts, 15th ed., Tonbridge: Charities Aid Foundation, 1997

The Foundation Directory, 16th ed, New York: The Foundation Center, 1994 [American]

A Guide to Company Giving, 1995/96 edition, edited by David Casson, London: Directory of Social Change, 1995 (new edition due spring 1997)

A Guide to the Major Trusts, 1995-96 edition
Vol 1: the top 300 trusts, edited by Luke Fitzherbert *et al.*, London: Directory of Social Change, 1995 (new edition due spring 1997)
Vol 2: 700 further trusts, edited by Paul Brown and David Casson, London: Directory of Social Change, 1995 (new edition due spring 1997)

The Handbook of Grants: A Guide to Sources of Public Funding for Museums, Galleries, Heritage & Visual Arts Organisations, Maggie Heath and Graeme Farnell, Milton Keynes: Museum Development Co., 1993

Some other useful publications:

D F Burlinghame, Fund-Raising as a Key to the Library's Future, *Library Trends*, vol. 42 no. 3 (1994), pp. 467-477

H Buxton, S Bell, Two contributions to the *Library Association Record* on project management in libraries, vol. 98 No. 8 (1996), pp. 410—413

IR 113 Gift Aid A Guide for Donors & Charities, Inland Revenue, September 1990

J C Potts, V D P Roper, Sponsorship and Fundraising in Public Libraries, *New Library World*, vol. 96 No. 1118 (1995), pp. 13-22